Guide to FRENCH Idioms

Also in this series,

Guide to FRENCH Idioms

Guide des locutions FRANÇAISES

P. Lupson

M.L. Pélissier

Printed on recyclable paper

PASSPORT BOOKS
a division of *NTC Publishing Group*
Lincolnwood, Illinois USA

1995 Printing

This edition first published in 1987 by Passport Books, a division of NTC Publishing Group,
4255 West Touhy Avenue, Lincolnwood (Chicago), Illinois 60646-1975 U.S.A.,
which has been granted exclusive publishing rights in North America and non-exclusive rights
to sell copies elsewhere. Originally published in the United Kingdom
by Stanley Thornes (Publishers) Ltd. ©1986 P. Lupson and Michel
Pélissier. All rights reserved. No part of this book may be reproduced,
stored in a retrieval system, or transmitted in any form or by any means,
electronic, mechanical, recording or otherwise, without the prior
permission of NTC Publishing Group.
Manufactured in the United States of America.

5 6 7 8 9 ML 9 8 7 6

Introduction

This book aims at providing a reference tool for all students of French, whether in high schools, in universities, or in evening classes. It will also be of value to others who simply want to enrich their knowledge of, and feel for, the French language.

Idioms can be a most rewarding aspect of language study, offering a fascinating glimpse into ways of thinking that are unique to a particular language community. It is this uniqueness that frequently makes it impossible to translate them literally. French idioms often conjure up a picture that has no discernible connection with their English meaning. For instance, one would hardly guess that the expression "tomber dans les pommes" (literally, "to fall into the apples") means "to faint" or "to pass out." Nor could one guess that "jeter un pavé dans la mare" (literally, "to throw a cobblestone into the pond") actually means "to cause an uproar." When the French hit a snag, they "fall on a bone" ("tomber sur un os"), and they don't go window-shopping but window-licking ("faire du lèche-vitrine")! The French language contains many such expressions, and they are one of the sources of its richness and fascination.

Idioms tend to be used strategically; that is, they capture and express the feelings and observations of a speaker, at times when maximum effect is desired with a minimum of language. An appreciation of their content and a sensitivity to the nuances they take on in certain contexts are, therefore, a mark of competent language use.

This book contains over 500 of the most commonly used idioms in the French language. They are the kind that can be used without embarrassment in any social circle! However, in instances where a particular idiom is most often encountered in informal conversation, it has been identified by the abbreviation "coll." (for colloquial). Idioms that are not specially marked can be used in any context. It does not always follow that an informal French idiom has an informal English equivalent, or vice versa. For this reason the abbreviation "coll." is also shown next to English equivalents where their use is more restricted than that of the French idiom.

For easy reference the idioms in this book are grouped within clearly defined subject areas and listed alphabetically in those areas. Example sentences in French, along with their English translations, illustrate the use of each idiom in context. In instances where a literal translation of the French bears little or no resemblance to the English meaning, a note on the origin of the French idiom has been added wherever possible.

The book can be used in a number of ways:

(a) using the Table of Contents at the front of the book, to discover idioms that are appropriate to a particular subject area;

(b) using the index of key French words, to track down the precise form of a particular half-remembered idiom;

(c) using the index of English idioms, to establish whether there is (or, in some cases, is not) an equivalent in French; and if so, whether it may be used in the same range of contexts as the English expression.

P.L.
M.L.P.

Acknowledgments

The authors would like to express their gratitude to the French Consulate, Liverpool, for valuable assistance in locating sources of information concerning the origins of many of the idioms.

Our grateful thanks also to Yannick Aubin and Josette Chipchase for checking the manuscript, and for their many helpful suggestions.

For Evelyn, Karen, and Michael-P.L.

For Sue, Christophe, and Daniel-M.L.P.

Contents

SUBJECT AREAS

▬ 1. ADMINISTRATION, ORGANIZATION ▬

CARTE

donner carte blanche à quelqu'un

to give someone a free hand

Quelle bonne nouvelle! Le Directeur général m'a appelé dans son bureau et m'a donné carte blanche pour lancer le nouveau projet.
What great news! The managing director called me into his office and gave me a free hand to launch the new project.

CHINOISERIE

chinoiseries administratives

red tape

Il a évité toutes les chinoiseries administratives en s'adressant directement à un ami qui travaillait dans ce service.
He cut through all the red tape by going directly to a friend who worked in that department.

PIED

mettre sur pied

to set up

Ils ont pris de longs mois pour mettre sur pied leur expédition dans l'Himalaya.
They took many months to set up their expedition to the Himalayas.

PLUIE

faire la pluie et le beau temps

to run the show

Notre sous-directeur fait la pluie et le beau temps. C'est lui qui prend toutes les décisions importantes, et pas le directeur.
Our assistant manager runs the show. He makes all the important decisions, not the manager.

▬ 2. AFFRONTS, INSOLENCE ▬

COURIR

Tu peux toujours courir! (coll.)

You can take a running jump! (coll.) *You can take a flying leap!* (coll.)

Pas question que je te fasse ta composition. Tu peux toujours courir!
No way am I going to do your essay for you. You can take a running jump!

ŒIL

se mettre le doigt dans l'œil

to have another think coming

Tu te mets le doigt dans l'œil si tu crois que je vais te prêter 5.000 francs. Tu m'en dois déjà assez.
You've got another think coming if you believe I'm going to lend you 5,000 francs. You already owe me enough.

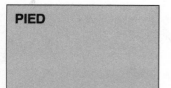

PIED

faire un pied de nez à quelqu'un

to thumb one's nose at someone

Jean-Paul est très polisson. Tu devrais lui parler; je l'ai vu faire un pied de nez à son grand-père.
Jean-Paul is very naughty. You ought to speak to him — I saw him thumb his nose at his grandfather.

REGARDER

Occupez-vous de ce qui vous regarde!

Mind your own business!

Non, je ne vous dirai pas combien il y a dans mon compte en banque. Occupez-vous de ce qui vous regarde!
No, I won't tell you how much there is in my bank account. Mind your own business!

TOUPET

avoir du toupet (coll.)

to have nerve (coll.)

Il a du toupet. Comment ose-t-il me redemander de l'argent alors qu'il n'a même pas commencé à me rembourser ce qu'il me doit déjà.
He's got nerve. How dare he ask me for money again when he hasn't even started paying me back what he already owes me.

3. AGE

FRISER

friser la cinquantaine

to be going on fifty

Pour quelqu'un qui frise la cinquantaine, il fait beaucoup de sport. Parfois je pense qu'il en fait trop.
For someone who's going on fifty, he's very active in sports. At times I think he overdoes it.

SONNER

avoir quarante ans bien sonnés (coll.)

to be on the far side of forty (coll.)

Bien qu'elle ait l'air beaucoup plus jeune, elle a en fait quarante ans bien sonnés.
Although she looks years younger, she is in fact on the far side of forty.

4. ALTERNATIVES, OPPOSITES, RECIPROCITY

BALLE

La balle est dans son camp.

The ball is in his court.

Je lui ai expliqué exactement comment faire amende honorable. A présent la balle est dans son camp.
I've explained to him exactly what he has to do to make amends. Now the ball is in his court.

MANCHE

C'est une autre paire de manches. (coll.)

It's a different kettle of fish. It's quite a different matter. That's another story.

En public cet homme politique semble généreux et aimable, mais chez lui c'est une autre paire de manches. Il est invivable.
That politician appears generous and kind in public, but at home with his family it's quite a different matter. He's impossible to live with.

Origin: **Sleeves were for many centuries removable and could be changed to suit particular occasions. Thus a change of sleeves meant a change of appearance, hence the idea of something completely different.**

MÉDAILLE

le revers de la médaille

the other side of the coin

Il est vrai que la baisse du franc favorise nos exportations, mais le revers de la médaille est que les importations nous coûtent davantage.
It's true that a weak franc boosts our exports but the other side of the coin is that imports cost more.

TRANCHANT

C'est à double tranchant.

It cuts both ways.

C'est à double tranchant. Tu dis que ton professeur n'est pas bon, mais comment veux-tu qu'il t'inspire si tu n'écoutes pas?
It cuts both ways. You say your teacher is poor, but how can you expect him to inspire you if you won't listen?

VOIR

Cela n'a rien à voir avec

It has nothing to do with

Il prétend qu'il l'aime simplement pour elle-même et que cela n'a rien à voir avec sa fortune.
He claims that he likes her for herself and that it has nothing to do with her fortune.

5. ANGER, ANNOYANCE, IRRITATION

BOL

en avoir ras le bol (coll.)

to be fed up with something, to be sick of something
(coll.)

J'en ai ras le bol de tes promesses. Pourquoi ne fais-tu pas
quelque chose pour changer?
I'm sick of all your promises. Why don't you actually do something
for a change?

BOULE

Cela me met en boule. (coll.)

It gets my goat. (coll.) It makes me mad. (coll.)

Cela me met en boule d'apprendre qu'on va construire une
nouvelle route à travers cette magnifique forêt.
It makes me mad to hear that a new road is going to be built through
that beautiful forest.

BOUQUET

C'est le bouquet!

That's the last straw! (coll.)

C'est le bouquet! Hier elle a perdu les clés de sa voiture et
aujourd'hui ce sont celles de l'appartement.
That's the last straw! Yesterday she lost the car keys and today it's
the keys to the apartment.

DOS

en avoir plein le dos

to be fed up with something

J'en ai plein le dos de tout ce boulot et de tous ces soucis. Je
crois que je vais démissionner.
I'm fed up with all this work and all this worry. I think I'm going to
resign.

FREIN

ronger son frein

to chomp at the bit, to be impatient

Il ronge son frein. D'abord il y a eu du retard pour le permis
de construire et puis le mauvais temps l'a empêché de
commencer.
He's chomping at the bit. First there was a delay with the building
permit and then the bad weather prevented him from getting
started.

HARICOT

C'est la fin des haricots! (coll.)

That's the last straw! (coll.)

Le mois passé c'était l'embrayage, à présent la boîte de vitesses. C'est la fin des haricots!
Last month it was the clutch, now it's the gearbox. That's the last straw!

MINE

faire grise mine

to look grumpy, to look anything but pleased

Robert a fait grise mine quand il a appris que St. Etienne avait perdu son match de coupe.
Robert looked anything but pleased when he heard that St. Etienne had lost the championship game.

PIQUER

piquer une crise (coll.)

to go through the roof (coll.)

Sa mère a piqué une crise quand Stéphane est revenu du coiffeur le crâne rasé.
His mother went through the roof when Stéphane came back from the barber with his head shaved.

PROMENER

envoyer promener

to send packing (coll.)

Quand il lui a demandé de l'embrasser, elle l'a envoyé promener.
When he asked her to kiss him, she sent him packing.

RÂLER

Ça fait râler. (coll.)

It makes you fume. It makes you mad. (coll.)

C'est Guillaume qui a fait toutes les recherches mais c'est son professeur qui s'en est attribué le mérite. Ça fait râler.
It's William who did all the research but his professor took the credit. It makes us fume.

Origin: **From the primary meaning of "râler," which is "to give the death rattle."**

6. APPEARANCE, DESCRIPTION

CROQUER

être belle à croquer

to be as pretty as a picture

Ta nouvelle robe te va à merveille, Karen. Tu es belle à croquer.
Your new dress really suits you, Karen. You're as pretty as a picture.

CHEVEU

les cheveux en bataille

dishevelled hair

Pauvre Josette! Elle a passé des heures à se préparer pour aller au théâtre, mais elle y est arrivée les cheveux en bataille à cause du vent.
Poor Josette! She spent ages getting herself ready to go to the theater, but she arrived with dishevelled hair because of the wind.

CHAMP

Le champ est libre.

The coast is clear.

Nous pouvons nous cacher dans cette cabane jusqu'à ce que le champ soit libre. Personne ne sait que nous sommes ici.
We'll be able to hide in this hut until the coast is clear. No one knows we're here.

CLOU

un vieux clou (coll.)

a lemon (coll.)

Tu crois peut-être avoir fait une bonne affaire, mais je suis sûr que c'est un vieux clou qu'on t'a vendu.
Maybe you think you've got a bargain, but I'm sure you've been sold a lemon.

DESSUS

mettre sens dessus dessous

to turn upside down

Quel désordre dans l'appartement. Les cambrioleurs avaient tout mis sens dessus dessous.
What a mess in the apartment. The burglars had turned everything upside down.

GUILLOTINE

une fenêtre à guillotine

a sash window

Ce n'est que dans les vieilles maisons qu'on trouve encore des fenêtres à guillotine.
It's only in old houses that you still find sash windows.

JAUNE

rire jaune

to give a sickly smile

Elle a ri jaune quand elle s'est rendu compte que sa plaisanterie avait raté et qu'elle devrait expliquer le tout à la directrice.
She gave a sickly smile when she realized that her joke had misfired and that she would have to explain everything to the principal.

Origin: **"Jaune" here represents the dull yellow of sulphur associated with hell. It came to represent betrayal and treachery. In the Middle Ages, Judas was depicted as wearing this particular color. Even in modern French the traditional association of "jaune" with betrayal is evident in the term "un jaune" meaning "a strikebreaker."**

JOUR

comme le jour et la nuit

as different as night and day

Ils ont beau être frères, ils sont comme le jour et la nuit. Ils ne sont d'accord sur rien.
They may be brothers, but they're as different as night and day. They can't agree on anything.

MINE

avoir une mine de papier mâché

to look washed out, to look like death warmed over (coll.)

Pauvre Danielle, elle a une mine de papier mâché. Ce dont elle a besoin ce sont de longues vacances au soleil.
Poor Danielle, she looks like death warmed over. What she needs is a long vacation in the sun.

MYOPE

myope comme une taupe

as blind as a bat

Il est myope comme une taupe sans ses lunettes.
He's as blind as a bat without his glasses.

NAGE

être en nage

to be covered with sweat (coll.), *to be bathed in perspiration*

Tu n'aurais pas dû garder ton gros pull pour jouer au football avec tes copains. Regarde, tu es tout en nage.
You shouldn't have kept your heavy sweater on to play soccer with your friends. Just look at you, all covered with sweat.

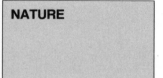

nature morte

still life

Je préfère de loin les paysages ou les portraits aux natures mortes.
I far prefer landscapes and portraits to still lifes.

un nid de poule

a pothole (in the street)

Cette route est terrible. Elle est si plein de nids de poules que ça vous fait sauter de votre siège.
This road is awful. It's so full of potholes that you get shaken out of your seat.

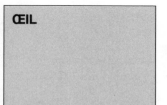

un œil au beurre noir

a black eye

Il mérite un œil au beurre noir pour toutes ses insultes.
He deserves a black eye for all his insults.

Origin: **"Beurre noir" is melted butter that has been allowed to go black. In the idiom it refers to the bruise that appears around an injured eye.**

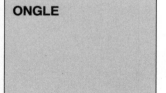

jusqu'au bout des ongles

to the fingertips, to the core

Elle est professeur jusqu'au bout des ongles. Même en vacances elle est à la recherche de matériel qu'elle peut utiliser en classe!
She's a teacher to her fingertips. Even on vacation she's on the lookout for material to use in class!

trempé jusqu'aux os

soaked to the skin

Il a plu si fort que même avec nos parapluies nous étions trempés jusqu'aux os.
It rained so heavily that even with our umbrellas we were soaked to the skin.

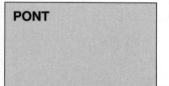

un pont en dos d'âne

a humpbacked bridge

Il faut toujours ralentir à l'approche d'un pont en dos d'âne. On ne sait jamais ce qui peut se trouver de l'autre côté.
You should always slow down as you come to a humpbacked bridge. You never know what's on the other side.

QUEUE

à la queue leu-leu

in single file

Les sept alpinistes avançaient à la queue leu-leu le long de l'arête étroite.
The seven climbers advanced along the narrow ridge in single file.

Origin: **The expression was originally "à la queue du loup" representing the way in which wolves followed each other in single file. "Leu" is simply an old spelling of "loup." The doubling of the word "leu" is due to a spelling error that originated in Picardy when "la queue de leu" (="la queue du loup") became "la queue leu leu."**

RÉGLÉ

réglé comme du papier à musique

as regular as clockwork

C'est réglé comme du papier à musique. La première chose qu'il fait en se levant est d'aller voir s'il y a du courrier.
It's as regular as clockwork. The first thing he does when he gets up is to see if there is any mail.

Origin: **The reference is to the well-marked, regular pattern of lines on sheet music.**

SUCRE

être tout sucre tout miel

to be all sweetness and light

Elle sait être tout sucre tout miel quand elle veut quelque chose.
She can be all sweetness and light when she wants something.

TAMBOUR

sans tambour ni trompette

without any fuss

Elle a quitté son poste sans tambour ni trompette après trente ans de présence. Elle n'a même pas voulu de réunion d'adieu.
She left her job without any fuss after thirty years. She didn't even want a farewell party.

TÊTE

une drôle de tête

You should have seen his face.

Les deux cambrioleurs ont fait une drôle de tête quand ils se sont rendu compte qu'ils étaient dans une maison vide!
You should have seen the faces of the two burglars when they realized they were in an empty house!

un trou (coll.)

a dump (coll.), *a hole* (coll.)

Quel trou! Il n'y a pas d'épicerie, pas de boulangerie et il n'y a même pas de café.
What a dump! There's no grocery, no bakery, and there isn't even a café.

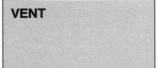

avoir du vent dans les voiles

to be tipsy

Tu es sûr qu'il n'a bu qu'une bière? Il a du vent dans les voiles.
Are you sure he's only drunk one beer? He's tipsy.

7. ARGUMENT, DISAGREEMENT

couper les cheveux en quatre

to split hairs

Inutile de couper les cheveux en quatre. Qu'il soit indien ou africain, c'est toujours un éléphant.
There's no need to split hairs. Whether it's Indian or African — it's still an elephant!

avoir maille à partir avec quelqu'un

to have a bone to pick with someone

Le délégué syndical a eu maille à partir avec le patron à propos de la longueur de la pause de midi
The union representative had a bone to pick with the boss about the length of the lunch break.

Origin: **"Une maille" was an old copper coin, and "partir" derives from "partager." Hence to have a "maille" to share meant that one possessed something that could be haggled over.**

une pomme de discorde

a bone of contention

Les aboiements incessants du chien sont vite devenus une pomme de discorde entre les voisins.
The dog's continual barking soon became a bone of contention between the neighbors.

Origin: **Referring to the apple given by Paris to Venus, which aroused the hatred of Juno and Minerva.**

8. ASSESSMENT, EVALUATION, ESTIMATION

CHACUN

tout un chacun

every Tom, Dick, and Harry

Autrefois c'était un club très fermé, mais de nos jours ils laissent entrer tout un chacun.
At one time this was an exclusive club, but now they let in every Tom, Dick, and Harry.

COMME

comme ci comme ça

fair to middling (coll.), *so so* (coll.)

"Que penses-tu de la pièce d'hier soir à la télé?"
"Comme ci comme ça."
"What did you think of the play on TV last night?"
"So so."

POULS

se tâter le pouls

to hesitate, to weigh one's options

Je me tâte le pouls: une Citroën, une Renault ou peut-être une Ford?
I'm hesitating: a Citroën, a Renault, or perhaps a Ford?

TIENS

Un tiens vaut mieux que deux tu l'auras. (prov.)

A bird in the hand is worth two in the bush. (prov.)

Oui, bien sûr je pourrais gagner gros si je remettais en jeu ce que j'ai gagné, mais comme on dit, "Un tiens vaut mieux que deux tu l'auras."
Yes, of course I could win a lot if I bet what I have already won, but as they say, "A bird in the hand is worth two in the bush."

VUE

à vue de nez

at a rough guess

A vue de nez je dirais qu'il a une trentaine d'années.
At a rough guess I would say he's about thirty.

9. ATTITUDE, OUTLOOK

BÊTE

chercher la petite bête

to nitpick

Que d'histoires pour une si petite faute d'orthographe! Vous cherchez toujours la petite bête.
So much fuss about a single spelling mistake! You're always nitpicking.

BRANCHÉ
CÂBLÉ
VENT

branché (coll.)

câblé (coll.)

dans le vent (coll.)

trendy (coll.), *with it* (coll.), *in* (coll.)

Jean-Claude se veut branché. Il essaie de se tenir au courant de tout: la mode, les disques, le ciné etc.
Jean-Claude likes to think of himself as trendy. He tries to keep up-to-date with everything: fashion, records, movies, etc.

CHAUD

Cela ne me fait ni chaud ni froid.

I'm not at all bothered.

Cela ne me fait ni chaud ni froid d'apprendre que la France n'est pas qualifiée pour la Coupe du Monde. Je ne m'intéresse pas au football.
I'm not bothered at all to hear that France hasn't qualified for the World Cup. I'm not interested in soccer.

CHEMISE

s'en moquer comme de sa première chemise (coll.)

not to give a hoot (coll.)

Je me moque de ce qu'il pense comme de ma première chemise. Il n'y connaît rien en politique.
I don't give a hoot about what he thinks. He doesn't know a thing about politics.

CHEVAL

être à cheval sur les principes

to be a stickler for principles

Le patron est à cheval sur les principes. Quand il dit "Défense de fumer ici," cela s'applique à tout le monde, y compris son fils.
The boss is a stickler for principles. When he says "No smoking here," that applies to everyone, including his son.

CUISSE

se croire sorti de la cuisse de Jupiter

to think a lot of oneself

Il se croit sorti de la cuisse de Jupiter. Il est convaincu que toutes les femmes l'adorent.
He thinks a lot of himself. He's convinced that every woman adores him.

DENT

serrer les dents

to keep a stiff upper lip

On dit que les Anglais montrent moins leurs émotions que les autres Européens. Même quand tout va mal, ils savent serrer les dents.
It's said that the English show their feelings less than other Europeans. Even when things go wrong, they know how to keep a stiff upper lip.

SE FICHER

se ficher de quelqu'un/quelque chose

couldn't care less about someone/something (coll.), *not to give a hoot for someone/something* (coll.)

Roger a échoué à son examen, mais il s'en fiche complètement.
Roger failed his exam, but he couldn't care less about it.

MIDI

chercher midi à quatorze heures

to look for complications

Pourquoi cherches-tu midi à quatorze heures? Le contrat. me semble tout à fait acceptable.
Why look for complications? The contract seems perfectly acceptable to me.

MONTAGNE

s'en faire une montagne

to make a mountain out of a molehill

Ne t'en fais pas une montagne. Je sais que ton professeur a critiqué ton dernier essai mais cela ne veut pas dire que tu vas échouer à ton examen.
Don't make a mountain out of a molehill. I know our teacher critized your last essay but that doesn't mean you're going to fail your exam.

ŒIL

fermer les yeux (sur)

to turn a blind eye (to)

Quand le douanier a regardé dans le coffre, il a vu que nous avions une bouteille en trop. Allait-il fermer les yeux?
When the customs officer looked in the trunk, he saw that we had one bottle too many. Would he turn a blind eye?

OURS

vendre la peau de l'ours avant de l'avoir tué (prov.)

to count one's chickens before they are hatched (prov.)

Ce n'est pas parce que tu as signé un contrat avec un éditeur que tu dois croire que tu es un grand auteur. Il ne faut pas vendre la peau de l'ours avant de l'avoir tué.
Just because you've signed a contract with a publisher, it doesn't mean you're a best-selling author. Don't count your chickens before they're hatched.

QUARANTE

s'en soucier comme de l'an quarante (coll.)

not to give a hoot (coll.)

Il se soucie comme de l'an quarante de son avenir et ne veut écouter les conseils de personne.
He doesn't give a hoot about his future and won't listen to anyone's advice.

Origin: **Used by monarchists to state that they were as worried about a particular problem as they were about the fortieth year in the French revolution, i.e., one that would never come.**

SOMMEIL

ne pas en perdre le sommeil pour autant

not to lose any sleep over it

On lui a dit que la compagnie allait faire faillite dans six mois, mais il n'en a pas perdu le sommeil pour autant. Il allait prendre sa retraite dans trois mois!
He was told that the company would be bankrupt in six months, but he didn't lose any sleep over it. He was retiring in three months!

TÊTE

en faire à sa tête

to go one's own way

Pourquoi ne veut-il écouter les conseils de personne? Il faut toujours qu'il en fasse à sa tête.
Why won't he listen to anyone's advice? He always has to go his own way.

VIE

voir la vie en rose

to see the world through rose-colored glasses

Mon oncle voit toujours la vie en rose. Bien qu'il sache qu'il va être licencié, il a prévu des vacances à l'étranger.
My uncle sees the world through rose-colored glasses. Even though he knows he's going to be fired, he's planned a vacation abroad.

10. ATTRIBUTES OF CHARACTER, PERSONAL QUALITIES

BOIS

Je vais vous montrer un peu de quel bois je me chauffe.

I'll show you what I'm made of.

Ah, ils n'ont pas voulu répondre à ma lettre de réclamations. Je vais leur montrer un peu de quel bois je me chauffe!
So they haven't answered my letter of complaint. I'll show them what I'm made of!

BREBIS

la brebis galeuse

the black sheep

C'est vraiment la brebis galeuse de la famille: ni diplômes, ni travail et le voici à présent en Cour d'Assise.
He's really the black sheep of the family: no qualifications, no job and now he's up before a court.

CHEVILLE

Personne ne lui arrive à la cheville.

He's head and shoulders above the rest. There's no one who can touch him.

Michel est le meilleur coureur que le club ait jamais eu. Personne ne lui arrive à la cheville.
Michel is the best cyclist the club has ever had. There's no one who can touch him.

CHIEN

avoir du chien (coll.)

to have a certain something (coll.)

Moi, si, je trouve qu'elle a du chien, ta copine. Elle est plutôt mignonne, tu sais.
Yes, I do think your friend has a certain something. She's rather cute, you know.

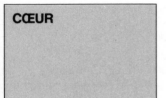

CŒUR

avoir le cœur sur la main

to be generous, giving

Eveline a le cœur sur la main. Elle vous donnerait son
dernier sou.
Eveline is very generous. She would give you her last penny.

D

utiliser le système D (coll.)

to be very resourceful

Il utilise le système D. Je ne sais pas comment il s'y prend
pour tout organiser si vite et si bien.
*He's very resourceful. I don't know how he manages to organize
everything so well and so quickly.*

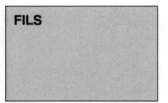

FILS

C'est bien le fils de son père.

He's a chip off the old block.

Tout comme son père avant lui, il veut conquérir des
sommets vierges. C'est bien le fils de son père.
*Like his father before him, he also wants to climb unconquered
mountains. He's a chip off the old block.*

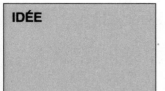

IDÉE

avoir de la suite dans les idées

to be single-minded

Je dois reconnaître que vous avez de la suite dans les idées.
Votre projet avance bien.
*I have to admit that you're very single-minded. Your project is
coming along well.*

NUMÉRO

Quel numéro!

What a character!

Il est toujours en retard, oublie quel jour c'est et n'arrive pas
au bon endroit. Quel numéro!
*He's always late, he forgets what day it is and he turns up at the
wrong place. What a character!*

ŒIL

ne pas avoir froid aux yeux

to have guts (coll.)

Elle n'a pas froid aux yeux. Moi, je n'aurais jamais osé aller demander un autographe au Président.
She has guts. I would never have dared to go and ask the President for his autograph.

PLUIE

ne pas être tombé de la dernière pluie

not to have been born yesterday

Allez raconter votre histoire à quelqu'un d'autre. Moi, je ne suis pas tombé de la dernière pluie. Je n'en crois pas un mot.
Go and tell someone else your story. I wasn't born yesterday. I don't believe a word of it.

POIL

avoir un poil dans la main (coll.)

to be an incredible lazybones

Impossible de lui faire faire quoi que ce soit. Il a un poil dans la main. Quel fainéant!
It's impossible to get him to do anything. He's an incredible lazybones. What a loafer!

POULE

une poule mouillée

a chicken (coll.), *yellow* (coll.), *a wimp* (coll.)

Quelle poule mouillée! Il ne tient tête à personne.
He's a real chicken! He never stands up to anyone.

SOUPE

être très soupe au lait

to fly off the handle easily, to be very quick-tempered

Faites très attention à votre façon de lui dire qu'il a tort. Il est très soupe au lait.
Be careful how you tell him he is wrong. He flies off the handle easily.

Origin: As with the parallel expression "monter comme une soupe au lait," the picture is of a pan of soup boiling over.

■■■■■■■■■ 11. BEHAVIOR ■■■■■■■

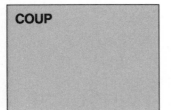

COUP

faire les quatre cents coups

to kick up one's heels

Pendant son adolescence, il a fait les quatre cents coups, mais à vingt ans il est soudain devenu le jeune homme sérieux que nous connaissons tous.
During his teens, he kicked up his heels, but at twenty he suddenly became the serious young man that we all know.

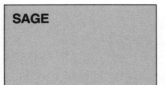

SAGE

sage comme une image

as good as gold

Toujours poli, travailleur; votre petit Christophe est sage comme une image.
Always polite, hardworking; your little Christopher is as good as gold.

■■■■■■ 12. BLUNTNESS, DIRECTNESS ■■■■■■

BLANC

dans le blanc des yeux

straight in the eye

Regarde-moi dans le blanc des yeux et redis-moi que tu ne l'as pas fait.
Look me straight in the eye and then tell me again you didn't do it.

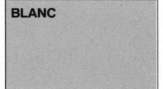

BUT

de but en blanc

point-blank, just like that (coll.)

Comment puis-je vous répondre de but en blanc? C'est une décision difficile. Je dois y mettre le temps qu'il faudra.
How can I give you an answer just like that? It's a difficult decision. I've got to take my time over it.

Origin: "But" derives from "la butte," the mound from which one fired a gun in shooting competitions. "Le blanc" was the target itself, i.e., a white bull's-eye.

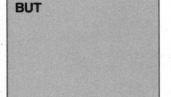

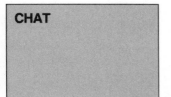

CHAT

appeler un chat un chat

to call a spade a spade

Sa femme a du tact. Lui, par contre, n'hésite pas à appeler un chat un chat.
His wife is tactful. He, on the other hand, doesn't hesitate to call a spade a spade.

CHEMIN

ne pas y aller par quatre chemins

to come straight to the point

Il n'y est pas allé par quatre chemins, et m'a dit que mon tableau était affreux.
He came straight to the point and told me my painting was terrible.

FRANC

avoir son franc parler

not to mince words

On lui a parfois reproché d'avoir son franc parler, mais chez un homme politique c'est plutôt une qualité à mon avis.
He has, at times, been criticized for not mincing words, but, for a politician, I think that's a rather positive quality.

MÂCHER

ne pas mâcher ses mots

not to mince words

Le professeur n'a pas mâché ses mots. Il a dit à Joséphine qu'elle était impolie, paresseuse et vaniteuse.
The teacher didn't mince words. He told Joséphine she was rude, lazy, and conceited.

QUATRE

dire à quelqu'un ses quatre vérités

to straighten someone out (coll.)

Il est grand temps que Paul lui dise ses quatre vérités. Elle ne peut pas continuer à traiter ainsi les gens.
It's time Paul straightened her out. She can't go on treating people like that.

13. BOREDOM

PIED

faire le pied de grue

to wait around, to cool one's heels

J'ai dû faire le pied de grue plus d'une heure. Où donc étais-tu?
I've had to wait around for more than an hour. Where have you been?

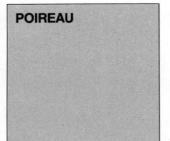

faire le poireau (coll.)

to be left cooling one's heels, to be left to wait around

On a manqué le train de quelques secondes et on a dû faire le poireau presque trois heures en attendant le suivant.
We missed the train by a few seconds and were left cooling our heels for nearly three hours while we waited for the next one.

Origin: **"Les poireaux" (leeks) remain in the ground longer than most other vegetables and can even be harvested after winter.**

être rasoir (coll.)

to be a bore

Qu'il est rasoir, Lucien. Il ne parle que de lui-même.
What a bore Lucien is. He only talks about himself.

Origin: **The picture is probably that of the boring, repetitive task of shaving.**

le train-train

humdrum routine

C'est toujours le même train-train au bureau. J'en ai plein le dos. Vivement les vacances!
It's always the same humdrum routine in the office. I'm fed up with it. I can't wait for vacation!

14. BUSYNESS

avoir d'autres chats à fouetter

to have other fish to fry, to have something more important to do

Je n'ai pas le temps de t'aider à ranger tes timbres. J'ai d'autres chats à fouetter. Dans une demi-heure ton père arrivera avec son patron.
I haven't got time to help you sort out your stamps. I've got something more important to do. In half an hour your father will be arriving with his boss.

PAIN

avoir du pain sur la planche (coll.)

to have a lot to do

Je voudrais bien aller au théâtre ce soir mais j'ai du pain sur la planche. Demain nous avons de la famille qui arrive du Canada et il me reste à préparer leurs chambres.
I would like to go to the theater tonight but I've got a lot to do. We have relatives arriving from Canada tomorrow and I've still got to get their rooms ready.

Origin: **Peasant farmers at one time used to make large quantities of bread that were stored on a board ("une planche"). To have bread in reserve later came to mean, by extension, that one had work in reserve, i.e., waiting to be completed.**

SAUT

faire un saut quelque part

to pop somewhere (coll.)

"Où est passée ta mère?"
"Elle est allée faire un saut en ville. Elle a dit qu'elle avait besoin de quelques provisions."
"Where has your mother gone?"
"She's popped into town. She said she needed some groceries."

TÊTE

ne pas savoir où donner de la tête

not to know where to start

Les courses, la lessive, la couture: j'ai tellement à faire que je ne sais pas où donner de la tête.
The shopping, the washing, the sewing: I have so much to do that I don't know where to start.

15. CARELESSNESS

brûler les étapes

to rush things

Voilà ce qui arrive quand on brûle les étapes. Le travail n'est ni fait ni à faire.
That's what happens when you rush things. The job is only half done.

ÉTAPE

JAMBE

faire quelque chose par dessous la jambe

to do something in a slipshod fashion

Le décorateur a fait ce travail par dessous la jambe. Quel gâchis!
The decorator has done this work in a slipshod fashion. What a mess!

Origin: **From "le jeu de paume," the forerunner of tennis. Occasionally a player would hit the ball under his legs for the amusement of the spectators.**

SIX

faire quelque chose à la six quatre deux

to do something in a slapdash way, to do something any old way (coll.)

Je vous avais demandé de vous appliquer. Alors, pourquoi avez-vous fait ce travail à la six quatre deux?
I told you to apply yourself. So why have you done this work any old way?

16. CAUTION, CAREFULNESS

ARGENT

ne pas prendre quelque chose pour argent comptant

to take something with a grain of salt

Ne prends pas ses promesses pour argent comptant. Il est rarement sincère.
Take his promises with a grain of salt. He rarely means what he says.

CHANDELLE

Le jeu n'en vaut pas la chandelle. (coll.)

It isn't worth it.

Le jeu n'en vaut pas la chandelle. Tu ne devrais pas essayer de passer la douane sans déclarer le cognac que tu as acheté en France.

Origin: **The reference was to insignificant winnings in a game of cards. It was said that they weren't even sufficient to pay for the cost of the candle that provided lighting for the players. This was particularly the case in homes of modest means where the players would leave a contribution towards the cost of providing candlelight for the game.**

CHAT

Chat échaudé craint l'eau froide. (prov.)

Once bitten twice shy. (prov.)

Je ne remangerai jamais ce plat, il m'a donné une indigestion terrible. Chat échaudé craint l'eau froide.
I'll never eat that dish again; it gave me terrible indigestion. Once bitten twice shy.

CHAT

ne pas réveiller le chat qui dort (prov.)

to let sleeping dogs lie (prov.)

Surtout ne parle pas de son passé douteux. Il ne faut pas réveiller le chat qui dort.
Make sure you don't dredge up his dubious past. You should let sleeping dogs lie.

CŒUR

en avoir le cœur net

to check

Je suis sûr que je leur ai renvoyé le formulaire. J'en aurai le cœur net. Quel est leur numéro de téléphone?
I'm sure I sent the form back to them. I'll check. What's their phone number?

LOUP

à pas de loup

stealthily

Pour ne pas être entendus par les gardes, les trois hommes avançaient à pas de loup.
So as not to be heard by the guards, the three men moved forward stealthily.

ŒIL

avoir/tenir quelqu'un à l'œil

to keep an eye on someone

Vous devrez la tenir à l'œil; elle a tendance à partir et à se perdre.
You'll have to keep an eye on her; she's liable to wander off and get lost.

POIRE

garder une poire pour la soif

to save something for a rainy day

Heureusement que j'avais gardé une poire pour la soif. L'auto a besoin d'un nouveau moteur!
It's a good thing I saved something for a rainy day. The car needs a new engine!

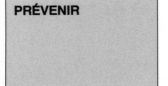

Mieux vaut prévenir que guérir. (prov.)

An ounce of prevention is worth a pound of cure. (prov.)

Il me faudra passer la nouvelle barrière au créosote. Mieux vaut prévenir que guérir.
I'll have to put wood preservative on the new gate. An ounce of prevention is worth a pound of cure.

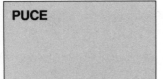

mettre la puce à l'oreille de quelqu'un

to arouse someone's suspicion

C'est le prix qui m'a mis la puce à l'oreille: cinquante francs pour une montre en or!
It was the price that aroused my suspicion: fifty francs for a gold watch!

17. CERTAINTY, CONVICTION

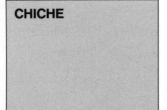

chiche que (coll.)

bet you (coll.)

"Chiche que je plonge du tremplin de six mètres."
"Ne fais pas l'imbécile. Tu n'as même jamais plongé de celui de trois mètres."
"Bet you I dive from the six meter board."
"Don't be stupid. You've never even dived from the three meter board."

Je n'en mettrais pas la main au feu.

I couldn't swear to it.

Je suis assez sûr d'avoir vu ton nom sur la liste, mais je n'en mettrais pas la main au feu.
I'm fairly certain I saw your name on the list, but I couldn't swear to it.

Origin: **From the medieval practice of establishing innocence or guilt according to the degree of burn suffered by a person who had been made to place a hand in fire as a means of judgment.**

en donner sa tête à couper

to bet one's life on it (coll.)

Je suis sûr que c'est le Président que j'ai vu hier. J'en donnerais ma tête à couper.
I'm sure it was the President I saw yesterday. I'd bet my life on it.

■■■■ 18. CHANGE, TRANSFORMATION ■■■■

BALANCE

faire pencher la balance en faveur de/au détriment de

to tip the scales in favor of/against

Bordeaux était en train de gagner le match, mais une mauvaise décision de l'arbitre a fait pencher la balance en faveur de Paris St. Germain qui a remporté la victoire.
Bordeaux was winning the game, but a bad decision by the referee tipped the scales in favor of Paris St. Germain, who won.

EAU

mettre de l'eau dans son vin

to mellow

Il a mis de l'eau dans son vin. A présent il est beaucoup plus calme et réfléchi.
He's mellowed. Nowadays he's a lot more quiet and reflective.

FUSIL

changer son fusil d'épaule

to change sides

Comment faire confiance à cet homme politique? Il a encore changé son fusil d'épaule!
How can you trust that politician? He's changed sides again!

PEAU

faire peau neuve

to turn over a new leaf

Vous ne le reconnaîtriez pas; il a fait peau neuve. Très organisé, toujours à l'heure, le sourire aux lèvres . . . Quelle transformation!
You wouldn't know him; he's turned over a new leaf. Very organized, always punctual, a smile on his face . . . What a transformation!

TABLE

faire table rase

to make a clean sweep

Le Premier Ministre a fait table rase et a complètement changé le Cabinet des Ministres.
The Prime Minister made a clean sweep and completely changed the Cabinet.

19. CLOTHES

CRI

le dernier cri

the latest fashion

Elle porte toujours des vêtements qui sont le dernier cri. Cela doit lui coûter une fortune!
She always wears clothes that are the latest fashion. It must cost her a fortune!

ÉPINGLE

tiré à quatre épingles

dressed to kill

Il est toujours tiré à quatre épingles. Il espère être élu maire et il soigne son image.
He's always dressed to kill. He hopes to be elected mayor and he's cultivating his image.

Origin: **Similar to the term "pin money" in English. From the 14th to the 16th centuries, pins were an item of luxury; and during this time husbands would give their wives money to buy pins for their dresses.**

JUSTE

un peu juste

a rather tight fit

J'aime beaucoup cette jupe mais elle est un peu juste. Avez-vous la taille au-dessus?
I like this skirt a lot but it's a rather tight fit. Do you have a larger size?

PAPILLON

un nœud-papillon

a bow tie

Mais oui, tu dois mettre un nœud-papillon si tu portes ton smoking.
Oh yes, you have to put on a bow tie if you wear your tuxedo.

TRENTE ET UN

se mettre sur son trente et un

to dress to the teeth

Pour accueillir la vedette de cinéma il s'est mis sur son trente et un: costume sombre, chemise blanche, nœud-papillon.
To welcome the film star he dressed to the teeth: dark suit, white shirt, bow tie.

Origin: **Obscure, but possibly a distortion of "mettre sur soi son trentain"; "trentain" being the name of an old luxury cloth. Alternatively, it might derive from certain card games in which the player with 31 points was the winner.**

■ 20. COMMUNICATION, INFORMATION ■

BOUCHE

de bouche à oreille

by word of mouth

On a appris la nouvelle de bouche à oreille bien avant qu'elle ne paraisse dans les journaux.
We heard the news by word of mouth long before it appeared in the papers.

CHANTER

chanter (coll.)

to tell

Que me chantez-vous là? Votre histoire ne tient pas debout.
What's this you're telling me? Your story doesn't hold water.

COUP

donner/passer un coup de fil à quelqu'un (coll.)

to give someone a ring, to phone someone

Passe-lui un coup de fil. C'est tellement plus rapide qu'une lettre.
Give him a ring. It's so much quicker than a letter.

COURANT

être au courant

to be informed, to know about

Vous êtes au courant? Marcel et Janine ont fini par se marier. C'est Madame Dupuis qui me l'a appris.
Have you heard? Marcel and Janine finally got married. It was Madame Dupuis who told me.

DOIGT

Mon petit doigt me l'a dit.

A little bird told me.

Tu as encore été polisson. Mon petit doigt me l'a dit.
You've been naughty again. A little bird told me.

MORCEAU

manger le morceau (coll.)

to spill the beans (coll.), to talk (coll.)

Le gang avait mis sur pied la parfaite attaque de banque, mais l'un d'eux a mangé le morceau. Ils ont tous été arrêtés.
The gang had planned a perfect bank robbery, but one of them spilled the beans. They were all arrested.

SIGNE

faire signe du doigt/de la main à quelqu'un

to beckon someone

La secrétaire lui a fait signe de la main d'entrer dans le bureau du directeur de la banque.
The secretary beckoned him into the bank manager's office.

SOURCE

tenir quelque chose de bonne source

to have something on good authority

Je tiens cela de bonne source: notre Député a l'intention de démissionner.
I have it on good authority that our Congressman intends to resign.

TABLE

se mettre à table (coll.)

to talk, to spill the beans

Les policiers n'ont pas eu à le questionner longtemps. Il s'est vite mis à table et a donné le nom de ses complices.
The police did not have to question him for long. He soon spilled the beans and gave his accomplices' names.

VER

tirer les vers du nez à quelqu'un (coll.)

to worm something out of someone (coll.)

Avec toutes ses petites questions, elle a fini par vous tirer les vers du nez. Elle va répéter à tout le monde que votre femme attend un heureux événement.
Will all her little questions, she managed to worm it out of you. She'll go and tell everyone that your wife is expecting.

■■■ 21. CONVERSATION, SPEAKING ■■■

BÂTON

parler à bâtons rompus

to talk about this and that

Cela a été une soirée très agréable. Nous avons regardé des photos et parlé à bâtons rompus.
It was a pleasant evening. We looked at photographs and talked about this and that.

CHAT

avoir un chat dans la gorge

to have a frog in one's throat

Monsieur le Maire a des difficultés à prononcer son discours. Il a un chat dans la gorge. Allez lui chercher un verre d'eau.
The mayor is finding it difficult to make his speech. He has a frog in his throat. Get him a glass of water.

CHEVEU

avoir un cheveu sur la langue

to have a lisp

Il a un cheveu sur la langue et on a beaucoup de difficulté à comprendre certains de ses mots, comme par exemple "satisfaire."
He has a lisp and you have a lot of difficulty understanding certain words of his, like "satisfy" for example.

COQ

passer du coq à l'âne

to change the subject willy-nilly

C'est agaçant de lui parler. Elle n'écoute qu'à moitié et elle passe du coq à l'âne.
She is annoying to talk to. She only half listens and then changes the subject willy-nilly.

Origin: **The rooster and the donkey here represent topics that are totally unrelated.**

FIL

perdre le fil

to lose the thread

Cela a été une interview très ennuyeuse parce que le ministre perdait constamment le fil de la conversation.
It was a very boring interview because the minister continually lost the thread of the conversation.

Origin: **From the Greek legend in which Ariadne gave her lover Theseus a ball of thread to enable him to find his way out of the labyrinth.**

LANGUE

avoir la langue bien pendue

to have a glib tongue

Ta sœur a toujours quelque chose à dire. Elle a la langue bien pendue.
Your sister always has something to say. She's got a glib tongue.

LANGUE

l'avoir sur le bout de la langue

to be on the tip of one's tongue

J'ai son nom sur le bout de la langue, mais je n'arrive pas à m'en souvenir.
His name is on the tip of my tongue, but I just can't remember it.

MOT

un gros mot

a bad word, a dirty word

Où as-tu appris ce gros mot? Je ne veux plus jamais l'entendre. C'est compris?
Where did you learn that dirty word? I never want to hear it again. Do you understand?

MOUTON

Revenons à nos moutons.

Let's get back to the subject.

C'est très intéressant de t'entendre parler de tes vacances, mais revenons à nos moutons. Quand vas-tu finir ce travail pour moi?
It's very interesting to hear about your vacation, but let's get back to the subject. When are you going to finish that job for me?

PIE

bavard comme une pie (coll.)

a chatterbox

Tous ses professeurs se plaignent de la même chose — elle est bavarde comme une pie.
All her teachers complain about the same thing — she's a chatterbox.

22. DECEPTION, DISHONESTY

COUVERTURE

tirer la couverture à soi (coll.)

to take all the credit, to gain unfair recognition

Le nouveau projet était l'idée d'Arnaud, mais c'est Gilbert qui a tiré la couverture à lui et a commercialisé le nouveau moteur.
The new design was Arnaud's idea, but it's Gilbert who took all the credit and marketed the new engine.

HISTOIRE

C'est une histoire à dormir debout.

It's a cock-and-bull story. It's an unbelievable story.

Quelle histoire à dormir debout! Il a dit qu'il était dans la Résistance pendant la guerre alors qu'on sait très bien qu'il était du côté du gouvernement de Vichy.
What a cock-and-bull story! He says that he was in the Resistance during the war, but everyone knows that he supported the Vichy government.

NOIR

travailler au noir

to moonlight

Tous ces gens qui travaillent au noir aggravent le problème du chômage. On peut dire qu'ils volent le travail des autres.
All those people who moonlight aggravate the problem of unemployment. You could even say they are robbing other people of work.

Origin: **Associated with activities carried out on the "marché noir," i.e., the black market.**

POT

un pot-de-vin

bribe

On entend quelquefois parler de disc-jockeys qui acceptent un pot-de-vin pour lancer un nouveau disque.
You sometimes hear of disc jockeys who accept a bribe for promoting a new record.

SALADE

Quelle salade! (coll.)

What a pack of lies! (coll.)

Quelle salade! Personne ne croira ton histoire, mon vieux.
What a pack of lies! Nobody will believe your story, my friend.

VASEUX

une excuse vaseuse

a lame excuse

Il dit qu'il a perdu son match de tennis parce qu'il avait mal au ventre. Quelle excuse vaseuse! A vrai dire, c'est un mauvais perdant.
He claims he lost the tennis match because he had a stomachache. What a lame excuse! The truth is, he's a poor loser.

Origin: **"Vaseux" means "muddy." By extension, therefore, it has the meaning of "confused," "muddled," or "woolly."**

VESSIE

faire prendre à quelqu'un des vessies pour des lanternes

to pull the wool over someone's eyes

Pourquoi essayez-vous de me faire prendre des vessies pour des lanternes? N'importe qui peut voir que vous avez copié.
Why are you trying to pull the wool over my eyes? Anybody can see that you copied.

23. DESPAIR

NORD

perdre le nord (coll.)

to go to pieces

Quand il a appris que sa fille était parmi les victimes, il a perdu le nord.
When he learned that his daughter was among the victims, he went to pieces.

Origin: **Referring to the loss of orientation when one is unable to locate north on the compass.**

ROULEAU

être au bout de son rouleau

to be at the end of one's rope

On tourne en voiture depuis des heures et on n'a toujours pas trouvé où loger. Il fait presque nuit et je suis épuisé. Je suis au bout de mon rouleau.
We've been driving around for hours and we still haven't found accommodations. It's almost dark and I'm exhausted. I'm at the end of my rope.

Origin: **Before the appearance of books in the form that we now know them, it was common practice to stick single sheets together end-to-end and to roll them around a piece of ivory or wood. "Le rouleau" refers to such a roll of sheets.**

24. DIFFICULTIES, PROBLEMS, UNPLEASANT SITUATIONS

BOUCHON

un bouchon

a traffic jam

C'est toujours la même histoire sur les routes des vacances. A cause des bouchons, on perd des heures et on s'impatiente.
It's always the same story on the roads during vacation periods. You waste hours because of traffic jams and get impatient.

Origin: **The literal meaning of "un bouchon" is "a plug" or "a cork." By extension the word is used figuratively to mean "traffic jam."**

COULEUR

en faire voir de toutes les couleurs à quelqu'un

to give someone a hard time

Leur fils leur en fait voir de toutes les couleurs. Ils n'ont pratiquement aucun contrôle sur lui.
Their son gives them a hard time. They have hardly any control over him.

DRAP
PROPRE

être dans de beaux draps
me/te etc. voilà propre (coll.)

to be in a fine mess (coll.)

Nous sommes dans de beaux draps. Nous voilà propres. Pas de passeport, pas d'argent . . . Que faire?
We're in a fine mess. No passport, no money . . . What are we going to do?

Origin: **Both expressions are ironic. They intend the opposite of what is stated.**

ENSEIGNE

être logés à la même enseigne

to be in the same boat

En ce qui concerne l'inflation et le chômage, beaucoup de pays européens sont logés à la même enseigne.
As regards inflation and unemployment, a lot of European countries are in the same boat.

Origin: **"Une enseigne" is an inn or hotel sign. The implication is that the people lodging under the same sign (i.e., at the same inn or hotel) all share similar conditions.**

FIL

ne tenir qu'à un fil

to hang by a thread

Sa vie ne tient qu'à un fil. Les médecins ne savent pas s'il s'en sortira.
His life is hanging by a thread. The doctors don't know if he will pull through.

FOURMI

avoir des fourmis

to be asleep (a part of the body)

Je ne peux plus bouger. J'ai des fourmis dans les jambes.
I can't move. My legs are asleep.

HÉBREU

Pour moi, c'est de l'hébreu. (coll.)

It's all Greek to me. (coll.)

Ce document est plein de jargon juridique. Pour moi, c'est de l'hébreu.
This document is full of legal jargon. It's Greek to me.

Origin: **Referring to the fact that the Hebrew script and language appear to be extremely complicated to the non-native speaker.**

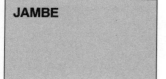

ne plus (se) tenir sur ses jambes

to be hardly able to stand

Je ne tiens plus sur mes jambes. Cette promenade en vélo était trop longue pour moi.
I can hardly stand. That bike ride was too much for me.

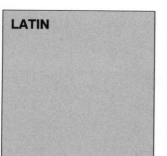

y perdre son latin

to be able to make neither head nor tail of something

C'est la troisième fois que j'essaie d'écrire ce programme pour mon ordinateur, mais c'est si compliqué que j'y perds mon latin.
It is the third time I have tried to write that computer program, but it is so complex that I can make neither head nor tail of it.

Origin: **A reference to the Latin student who faltered in the middle of a Latin speech because of a lack of vocabulary.**

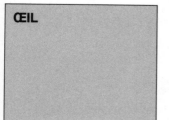

avoir les yeux plus grands que le ventre

to bite off more than one can chew

Tu as toujours les yeux plus grands que le ventre. Tu as voulu commencer ces trois tâches en même temps et à présent tu es complètement dépassé.
You always bite off more than you can chew. You wanted to start those three jobs at the same time and now you are completely swamped.

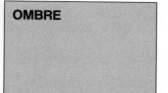

Il y a une ombre au tableau.

There's a fly in the ointment.

Nous espérons venir vous voir la semaine prochaine, mais il y a une ombre au tableau — notre voiture fait à nouveau des siennes.
We're hoping to come and see you next week, but there's a fly in the ointment — the car is acting up again.

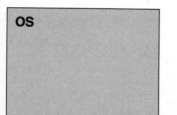

tomber sur un os

to hit a snag

J'espérais avoir réparé votre voiture pour aujourd'hui, mais malheureusement je suis tombé sur un os, et elle ne sera pas prête avant la semaine prochaine.
I had hoped to have the car repaired for you by today, but unfortunately I've hit a snag and it won't be ready until next week.

PAS

un mauvais pas

a tight spot

"Comment as-tu réussi à te tirer de ce mauvais pas?"
"Oh, c'est très simple. J'ai fait appel à tous mes amis."
"How did you manage to get out of that tight spot?"
"Oh, very simple. I asked all my friends to help me."

PÉTRIN

être dans le pétrin (coll.)

to be in a jam (coll.), *to be in a mess* (coll.), *to be in a fix* (coll.)

Le pauvre! Il est dans le pétrin. Il aura bien besoin de l'aide de tous ses amis.
The poor man! He's in a fix. He'll really need the help of all his friends.

SAINT

ne pas savoir à quel saint se vouer

not to know which way to turn

J'ai tout essayé. Je lui ai parlé longuement, je l'ai grondé, je l'ai puni. Rien n'y fait. Je ne sais plus à quel saint me vouer.
I've tried everything. I've talked to him at length; I've chided him and punished him. Nothing works. I no longer know which way to turn.

TROU

avoir un trou de mémoire

to have a lapse of memory, one's mind goes blank

Je connaissais le titre du livre mais je ne pouvais pas m'en souvenir. J'ai eu un trou de mémoire.
I knew the title of the book but I just couldn't remember it. My mind went blank.

VERT

en avoir vu des vertes et des pas mûres (coll.)

to have been through a lot (coll.), *to have seen it all* (coll.)

Vous savez, au cours de mes vingt ans dans la police j'en ai vu des vertes et des pas mûres. Cela ne fait aucun doute que la criminalité ne fait qu'augmenter.
You know, in my twenty years on the police force, I've seen it all. There's no doubt that crime is continually on the increase.

VINAIGRE

tourner au vinaigre

to turn sour

Les choses ont tourné au vinaigre quand l'arbitre a refusé le but. Les spectateurs l'ont hué et deux des joueurs ont commencé à se battre.
Things went sour when the referee disallowed the goal. The spectators booed him and two of the players started fighting.

25. DISCOMFORT, UNEASINESS

CHOSE

se sentir tout chose

to feel strange, to feel funny (coll.)

Je me suis senti tout chose quand on m'a dit que le directeur voulait me voir. Qu'est-ce que je pouvais avoir fait?
I felt strange when I was told that the boss wanted to see me. What could I have done?

PEAU

se sentir mal dans sa peau

to feel ill at ease

Il dit qu'il se sent mal dans sa peau chaque fois qu'il doit prononcer un discours.
He says he feels ill at ease each time he has to make a speech.

26. DISHARMONY BETWEEN PEOPLE

BÂTON

mettre des bâtons dans les roues

to throw a monkey wrench in the works

Il serait sans doute devenu Député mais ses adversaires lui ont mis des bâtons dans les roues en tirant un scandale de son passé.
He would probably have been elected to Congress but his opponents threw a monkey wrench in the works by dragging up some scandal from his past.

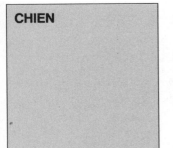

se regarder en chiens de faïence

to look daggers at each other, to glare at each other

Pourquoi avoir invité Christine et Sophie? Tu sais qu'elles se détestent. Pas surprenant qu'elles aient passé la soirée à se regarder en chiens de faïence.
Why did you invite Christine and Sophie? You know they detest each other. It's hardly surprising they spent the evening glaring at each other.

Origin: **The idea is that people on such terms show the same animosity as china dogs.**

garder une dent contre

to bear a grudge against

J'aimerais croire qu'elle m'a pardonné, mais je sens qu'elle me garde une dent.
I'd like to think that she has forgiven me, but I sense that she bears me a grudge.

foudroyer quelqu'un du regard

to glare at someone, to look daggers at someone, to give someone a withering look

Cela ne m'étonne pas que Simone t'ait foudroyé du regard. La personne sur qui tu faisais des commentaires désobligeants était son petit ami!
I'm not surprised Simone glared at you. The person you were making rude remarks about is her boyfriend!

battre froid à quelqu'un

to give someone the cold shoulder

Depuis que je lui ai dit que je n'avais pas envie de sortir avec lui, Thierry me bat froid.
Since I said I didn't want to go out with him, Thierry has given me the cold shoulder.

une grève du zèle

a work slowdown

Il y avait d'interminables files de voitures à cause d'une grève du zèle des douaniers.
There were endless lines of cars because of the customs officers' work slowdown.

PAVÉ

jeter un pavé dans la mare

to cause an uproar, to stir things up

Quel pavé dans la mare quand il a annoncé en public qu'il y avait un espion au sein du Cabinet!
He really caused an uproar when he publicly announced that there was a spy in the Cabinet itself!

QUARANTAINE

mettre en quarantaine

to give the silent treatment

Les grévistes ont mis en quarantaine ceux qui refusaient de se joindre à eux.
The strikers gave the silent treatment to all those who refused to join them.

Origin: **The first meaning of the expression is to "put into quarantine," that is to say, forty days' isolation. By extension it has come to mean "ignore."**

TOMBER

laisser tomber quelqu'un

to jilt someone, to drop someone

Dès qu'elle a appris qu'il était marié, elle l'a laissé tomber.
As soon as she found out he was married, she jilted him.

■■■ 27. DISLIKE, DISPLEASURE ■■■

BÊTE

C'est ma bête noire.

That's my pet peeve. I just can't stand it.

Sa bête noire, c'est l'utilisation du franglais par les journalistes.
His pet peeve is the use of franglais by journalists.

CŒUR

Cela me soulève le cœur.

i) *It makes me sick. (mental reaction)*

ii) *It turns my stomach. It makes me want to throw up. (physical reaction)*

i) Cela me soulève le cœur de les voir ainsi traiter leurs enfants.
    It makes me sick the way they treat their children.
ii) Quelle odeur terrible! Cela me soulève le cœur.
    What an awful smell! It turns my stomach.

GRIPPE

prendre quelqu'un en grippe

to take a sudden dislike to someone

Je l'ai pris en grippe dès l'instant où je l'ai entendu se vanter de ses exploits.
I took a sudden dislike to him when I heard him bragging about his great achievements.

Origin: **Antiphrasis. The original meaning of "grippe" was a "sudden fancy" and in the idiom it was used to express the exact opposite of this meaning.**

NEZ

avoir quelqu'un dans le nez (coll.)

to get on someone's nerves, to be unable to stand someone

André, je l'ai dans le nez. Chaque fois qu'il me voit, il tient absolument à me dire avec quel succès il s'occupe de ses affaires.
André gets on my nerves. Every time he sees me he insists on telling me how successfully he runs his affairs.

**SENTIR
VOIR**

**ne pas pouvoir sentir quelqu'un
ne pas pouvoir voir quelqu'un**

to be unable to stand someone

Je ne peux pas sentir/voir les hypocrites, ni les menteurs.
I can't stand hypocrites or liars.

28. DISTANCE

OISEAU

à vol d'oiseau

as the crow flies

Le sommet est à deux kilomètres à vol d'oiseau, mais par les sentiers sinueux à plus de neuf kilomètres.
The summit is two kilometers away as the crow flies, but following the winding paths it's more than nine.

VUE

à perte de vue

as far as the eye can see

Quand on traverse la Beauce on voit des champs de maïs et de blé à perte de vue.
When you go through the Beauce region you can see fields of corn and wheat as far as the eye can see.

29. DOMINANCE, OPPRESSION

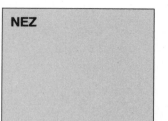

NEZ

mener quelqu'un par le bout du nez

to have someone under one's thumb, to henpeck someone

Sa femme le mène vraiment par le bout du nez. Il doit même lui demander la permission d'aller voir un match de football.
He's really henpecked by his wife. He even has to ask her permission to watch a soccer game.

CHANTER

faire chanter quelqu'un

to blackmail someone

Il a fait chanter cette famille pendant six mois avant d'être découvert par la police.
He blackmailed that family for six months before being discovered by the police.

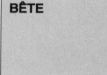

30. EASE, SIMPLICITY

BÊTE

C'est bête comme chou.

It's child's play. It's as easy as pie.

Au début cela peut sembler difficile de skier, mais tu verras, c'est bête comme chou.
Skiing can seem difficult at first, but you'll see, it's as easy as pie.

Origin: **The comparison refers to the homey simplicity of the humble cabbage.**

BONJOUR

simple comme bonjour

a piece of cake

Vous n'aurez aucun problème à faire de la planche à voile. Vous verrez, c'est simple comme bonjour.
You'll have no difficulty windsurfing. You'll see, it's a piece of cake.

MER

Ce n'est pas la mer à boire.

It's not as bad as all that.

Oui, bien sûr, on est un peu nerveux le jour du permis. Mais, tu verras, ce n'est pas la mer à boire.
Yes, of course, you're a little nervous the day of the driver's test. But you'll see, it's not as bad as all that.

31. EFFORT, EXERTION

BOUCHÉE

mettre les bouchées doubles

to work very hard, to work at twice the speed

Plus qu'un mois avant l'examen final. Il va me falloir mettre les bouchées doubles si je veux être prêt.
Only a month left before the final exam. I'm going to have to work at twice the speed if I want to be ready.

CHANDELLE

brûler la chandelle par les deux bouts

to burn the candle at both ends

Il brûle la chandelle par les deux bouts: huit heures au bureau, de sortie tous les soirs, et de plus il a son roman à finir!
He's burning the candle at both ends: eight hours at the office, out on the town every night, and on top of all that he's got his novel to finish!

COUP
PEINE

Ça vaut le coup.
Cela vaut la peine.

It's worth it. It's worth the trouble.

C'est vrai que l'apprentissage est long et difficile, mais cela vaut le coup/la peine. Quand ta formation sera terminée, tu verras que tu auras un bon métier.
It's true that the apprenticeship is long and hard, but it's worth it. When your training is finished, you'll find that you'll get a good job.

COÛTE

coûte que coûte

at all costs, come what may, whatever you do

Tu dois coûte que coûte prendre ton médicament. Je sais que tu n'aimes pas son goût, mais tu ne guériras pas sans ça.
You must take your medicine whatever you do. I know you don't like the taste, but you won't get better without it.

HALEINE

C'est un travail de longue haleine.

It's a long and exacting task.

On prend beaucoup de plaisir à apprendre une langue vivante, mais c'est un travail de longue haleine. Pour réussir on a besoin de persévérance.
It's great fun learning a foreign language, but it's also a long and exacting task. You'll need to persevere if you're going to succeed.

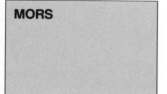

prendre le mors aux dents

to take the bull by the horns

Tu as hésité assez longtemps. Il va te falloir prendre le mors aux dents et lui demander un rendez-vous.
You've hesitated long enough. You'll have to take the bull by the horns and make an appointment with him.

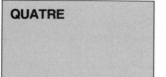

faire des pieds et des mains

to move heaven and earth

Il a fait des pieds et des mains pour obtenir un visa mais sans le moindre succès.
He moved heaven and earth to get a visa but without the slightest success.

se mettre en quatre

to go out of one's way

Il s'est mis en quatre pour recevoir sa belle-famille. Ils devraient être ravis de leur séjour.
He went out of his way to entertain his in-laws. They should be delighted with their stay.

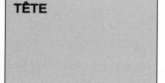

se casser la tête

to rack one's brains

Ne vous cassez pas la tête. Ce serait plus simple d'appeler un garage. Vous n'êtes pas mécanicien.
Don't rack your brains. It would be easier to call a garage. You're not a mechanic.

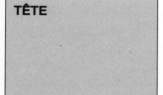

se creuser la tête

to rack one's brains

Je n'arrive pas à me rappeler où j'ai mis mon passeport. Je me suis creusé la tête pour essayer de penser à tous les coins possibles, mais en vain.
I just can't remember where I put my passport. I've racked my brains and tried to think of everywhere possible, but in vain.

32. ESCAPE, FLIGHT

prendre la clé des champs

to run off

Un lion s'est échappé du zoo et a pris la clé des champs. La police a prévenu le public d'être vigilant.
A lion has escaped from the zoo and run off. The police have warned the public to be vigilant.

CLOCHE

déménager à la cloche de bois

to skip out (coll.)

Ils n'avaient pas payé leur loyer depuis trois mois, et hier vers deux heures du matin ils ont déménagé à la cloche de bois.
They hadn't paid their rent for three months and yesterday about 2 a.m. they skipped out.

Origin: **The picture is of making as little noise as a wooden bell would make.**

COMPAGNIE

fausser compagnie à quelqu'un

to give someone the slip

Deux jours après son arrestation le criminel a faussé compagnie à la police.
Two days after his arrest the convict gave the police the slip.

ÉCOLE **SÉCHER**

faire l'école buissonnière
sécher les cours (coll.)

to play hooky (coll.), *to ditch school* (coll.)

Comment peut-on dissuader les élèves de faire l'école buissonnière/sécher les cours quand il fait si chaud et que les vacances sont si proches?
How can we dissuade the students from playing hooky when it's so hot and when vacation is so near?

JAMBES

prendre ses jambes à son cou

to take to one's heels

Ces deux jeunes voyous ont commencé à se faire menaçants. C'est alors que j'ai pris mes jambes à mon cou.
Those two young hooligans began to get threatening. That's when I took to my heels.

SAUVER

Sauve qui peut!

Every man for himself!

Regardez! Nous coulons! Sauve qui peut! La côte n'est pas loin.
Look! We're sinking! Every man for himself! The shore isn't far.

33. FACILITIES, CONVENIENCES

les clous

pedestrian crossing

Vous devez apprendre à votre jeune fils à traverser entre les clous. Sinon, il va se faire renverser un de ces jours.
You'll have to teach your young son to cross at the pedestrian crossing. If not, he'll be run over one of these days.

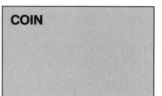

le petit coin (coll.)

the bathroom, the toilet

"Où se trouve le petit coin, s'il vous plait?"
"Au premier étage, à droite."
"Where is the bathroom, please?"
"On the first floor, on the right."

34. FAILURE

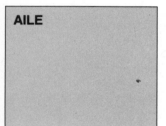

battre de l'aile

to flounder

Ils ont trop emprunté d'argent et mal calculé le marché pour leurs produits. Depuis quelques mois leur affaire bat de l'aile.
They borrowed too much money and misjudged the market for their products. Their business has been floundering these last few months.

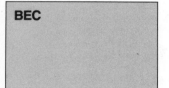

rester le bec dans l'eau

to be left high and dry

Les autres ont réussi à se tirer d'ennui en vendant leurs actions, mais lui est resté le bec dans l'eau.
The others managed to get out of trouble by selling their shares, but he was left high and dry.

BREDOUILLE

revenir bredouille

to come back empty-handed

C'est la troisième fois que je suis allé pêcher la truite dans ce ruisseau, mais à chaque fois je suis revenu bredouille.
It's the third time I've been trout fishing in that stream, but each time I've come back empty-handed.

Origin: **From the game of backgammon. It was possible for a player to "jouer bredouille," i.e., without letting his opponent gain a single point. The latter would then have completed the game "bredouille," without points, hence by extension, empty-handed.**

CHOU

faire chou blanc

to draw a blank

Les gendarmes ont fouillé l'apartement trois fois, mais à chaque fois ils ont fait chou blanc. Ils n'ont pas pu trouver les diamants volés.
The police searched the apartment three times, but each time they drew a blank. They couldn't find the stolen diamonds.

Origin: **Nothing to do with cabbage. The expression comes from a game resembling bowling when one said of a player who had failed to knock down any pins that he had "fait coup blanc." "Coup" was pronounced "choup" in the dialect of Berry, and it is from this that the present spelling of the idiom has developed.**

ÉPONGE

jeter l'éponge

to give up, to throw in the towel

Après s'être attaqué seul au problème pendant des heures, il a dû s'avouer vaincu et jeter l'éponge.
After tackling the problem on his own for hours, he had to admit he was beaten and he threw in the towel.

FORT

C'est plus fort que moi.

I can't help it.

C'est plus fort que moi, il faut que je grignote. Ce régime me démoralise;
I can't help it; I've got to have a bite to eat. This diet is getting me down.

FOUR

faire un four

to flop, to be a fiasco

Je ne comprends pas pourqoi son dernier film a fait un four pareil. Le scénario était bon et il avait réuni une excellente équipe.

I can't understand why his latest film has been such a flop. The script was good and he had gathered together an excellent team.

Origin: **Probably related to the idea of being black and empty "comme dans un four." "Faire four" was the expression used by actors to describe the darkness and emptiness of the theater when no spectators had turned up.**

JAMBE

Ça me fait une belle jambe! (coll.)

A lot of good it does me!

J'apprends le nouveau vocabulaire chaque fois. Ça me fait une belle jambe! J'ai toujours des résultats minables.
I learn the new vocabulary every time. A lot of good it does me! I always get useless results.

Origin: **The idiom dates from the 16th century when men abandoned "la robe" for "les chausses" thereby revealing their legs. At that time, their legs were seen as objects of interest and beauty in the way that women's legs were to become later. The idiom is an example of antiphrasis, the opposite really being meant.**

JEAN

être Gros-Jean comme devant

to be back to square one, to be no better off

Nous avons déménagé pour fuir nos bruyants voisins seulement pour découvrir que notre nouveau voisin joue de la trompette tous les soirs. Nous sommes Gros-Jean comme devant.
We moved to get away from our noisy neighbors only to find that our new neighbor practices his trumpet every evening. We're no better off.

Origin: **The expression derives from a character known in French tradition as Gros-Jean, an ordinary man of modest means who suffered continual disappointments.**

LANGUE

donner sa langue au chat

to give up

"Alors, tu ne vois vraiment pas de solution?"
"Non, je donne ma langue au chat. La devinette est trop dure pour moi."
"So, you really can't get the answer?"
"No, I give up. The riddle is too hard for me."

Origin: **The expression was formerly "au chien." It was replaced by "au chat" because the latter sounded less aggressive and more friendly for children who used the term in games and riddles. The idea is that without a tongue (eaten by the cat) one cannot give an answer.**

ŒUF

étouffer/tuer une idée dans l'œuf

to nip an idea in the bud

Il voulait sa propre enterprise, mais ses ennuis d'argent ont tué l'idée dans l'œuf.
He wanted his own business, but his money problems nipped the idea in the bud.

PIÈGE

se faire prendre à son propre piège

to get caught in one's own trap

L'homme politique s'est fait prendre à son propre piège. Sa campagne de diffamation contre son adversaire lui a fait perdre sa propre popularité.
The politician was caught in his own trap. His smear campaign against his opponents led to the loss of his own popularity.

POINT-MORT

être au point-mort

to be at a standstill

Depuis plus d'un mois les négociations sont au point-mort. Ni l'un ni l'autre ne veut céder.
For over a month the negotiations have been at a standstill. Neither side wants to make concessions.

Origin: **"Le point-mort" is the neutral gear of an engine.**

VESTE

prendre une veste (coll.)

to come a cropper (coll.), *to fail miserably*

Aux dernières législatives, Madame de Faite a pris une veste. Elle n'a obtenu que 3% des voix.
In the last elections, Madame de Faite came a cropper. She only won 3% of the votes.

Origin: **Obscure, but possibly a variation of "prendre une capote," an expression used when a player in a game of cards lost all the tricks. His embarrassment would have been equal to having a "capot" (later "capote") thrown over his head.**

ZÉRO

recommencer à zéro

to start from scratch

Ce papier peint n'est pas d'aplomb. Il va falloir l'enlever et recommencer à zéro.
This wallpaper isn't straight. We'll have to take it off and start from scratch.

35. FEAR

JAMBE

avoir les jambes en coton

one's legs turn to jelly

J'ai horreur de l'altitude. J'ai les jambes en coton quand je regarde en bas.
I'm terrified of heights. My legs turn to jelly when I look down.

PEUR

avoir une peur bleue de

to be scared to death of

Elle a une peur bleue des araignées. Elle prend ses jambes à son cou chaque fois qu'elle en voit une.
She's scared to death of spiders. She runs a mile whenever she sees one.

SANG

Mon sang n'a fait qu'un tour.

My heart skipped a beat.

Mon sang n'a fait qu'un tour quand j'ai vu mon fils de trois ans sur ce mur de plus de deux mètres de haut.
My heart skipped a beat when I saw my three-year-old son standing on that wall more than two meters high.

SUEUR

avoir des sueurs froides

to be in a cold sweat (coll.)

J'ai eu des sueurs froides quand j'ai regardé la liste des résultats. Je l'ai lue tellement vite que j'ai manqué mon nom la première fois.
I was in a cold sweat when I looked at the list of test results. I read it so quickly that I missed my name the first time.

TRAC

avoir le trac

to have stage fright

On voyait très bien que le jeune acteur avait le trac. Sa voix a tremblé tout au long de la première scène.
You could see very clearly that the young actor had stage fright. His voice trembled all the way through the opening scene.

Origin: **Either from "tracas" meaning worries, or from the chattering sound made by the teeth of a person who is in a state of fear.**

36. FOOD

ASSIETTE

une assiette anglaise

cold cuts

Que diriez-vous d'une assiette anglaise ce soir? Il fait trop chaud pour cuisiner.
What would you say about cold cuts this evening? It's too hot to cook.

BIFTECK

un bifteck bleu

a very rare steak

Lui, il demande toujours un bifteck bleu. Personnellement j'ai horreur de la viande peu cuite.
He always asks for a very rare steak. Personally I can't stand underdone meat.

CROÛTE

casser la croûte (coll.)

to have a snack

On va acheter du pâté et du pain et on cassera la croûte en route.
We'll buy some pâté and some bread, and we'll have a snack on the way.

FAIM

avoir une faim de loup

to be famished, to be starving

Je n'ai rien mangé depuis plus de douze heures. J'ai une faim de loup.
I haven't eaten for more than twelve hours. I'm starving.

FAIM

mourir de faim

to be starving

Je n'ai rien mangé depuis ce matin. Je meurs de faim!
I haven't eaten all morning. I'm starving!

FRUIT

des fruits de mer

seafood

Je peux vous recommander les fruits de mer. Ils sont vraiment délicieux.
I can recommend the seafood to you. It's really delicious.

LANGUE

une langue de chat

a ladyfinger

J'adore manger des langues de chat avec mon café.
I love eating ladyfingers with my coffee.

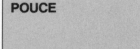

POINT

à point

medium

Comment voulez-vous votre bifteck? Saignant? A point?
Ou bien cuit?
How do you like your steak? Rare? Medium? Or well-done?

POMME DE TERRE

pommes de terre en robe de chambre/pommes de terre en robe des champs

baked potatoes

De la purée? Des frites? Ou préférez-vous des pommes de terre en robe de chambre/en robe des champs?
Some mashed potatoes? Some French fries? Or do you prefer baked potatoes?

POUCE

manger sur le pouce (coll.)

to grab a bite (coll.), *to have a quick snack*

Il nous reste une demi-heure avant le départ du train. On mange quelque chose sur le pouce?
We've got half an hour before the train leaves. Shall we grab a bite?

37. HAPPINESS, PLEASURE

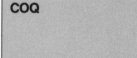

ANGE

être aux anges

to be on cloud nine (coll.), *to be ecstatic*

Quand Suzanne a appris qu'elle avait le poste, elle a été aux anges.
When Suzanne heard that she got the job, she was ecstatic.

CŒUR

s'en donner à cœur joie

to have a great time (coll.)

C'était si agréable de regarder les enfants s'en donner à cœur joie sur la plage. Ils ont très bien joué ensemble.
It was so nice to watch the children having a great time on the beach. They played very well together.

COQ

être comme un coq en pâte

to be in clover

Après des années de difficulté, son entreprise est devenue florissante. A présent il est comme un coq en pâte.
After years of hardship his business suddenly began to flourish. Now he's in clover.

GORGE

avoir la gorge serrée

to have a lump in one's throat

J'ai eu la gorge serrée quand je les ai vus réunis après tant d'années.
I had a lump in my throat when I saw them reunited after so many years.

POISSON

comme un poisson dans l'eau

in one's element

On avait un peu peur que notre fils n'ait des problèmes en changeant d'école, mais il est comme un poisson dans l'eau.
We were a bit concerned that our son might have problems when he changed schools, but he's in his element.

38. HARMONY BETWEEN PEOPLE

CHAPEAU

tirer son chapeau à quelqu'un

to take one's hat off to someone

Je lui tire mon chapeau. Il a fait beaucoup pour les pauvres et les indigents.
I take my hat off to him. He's done a lot for the poor and needy.

CHOU

mon petit chou

honey (coll.), *baby* (coll.)

Il a douze ans à présent. Sa mère ne devrait plus l'appeler "mon petit chou" devant ses copains.
He's twelve now. His mother shouldn't call him "baby" in front of his friends.

COUP

un coup de foudre

love at first sight

Cela a été un coup de foudre pour eux. Ils se sont mariés un mois après s'être rencontrés.
It was love at first sight for them. They married a month after they had met.

FRÈRE

vieux frère (coll.)

buddy (coll.), *pal* (coll.)

Salut vieux frère! Il y a longtemps qu'on ne s'était pas vus. Comment vas-tu?
Hi pal! Long time no see. How are you?

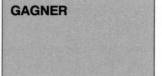

gagner à être connu

to grow on someone

Elle semble très ordinaire, mais vous verrez, elle gagne à être connue.
She seems pretty ordinary, but you'll see, she grows on you.

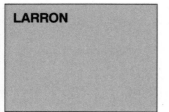

s'entendre comme larrons en foire

to be as thick as thieves

Ça ne sert à rien d'aller se plaindre au maire de la malhonnêteté de l'entrepreneur. Ils s'entendent comme larrons en foire.
It's no use complaining to the mayor about the builder's dishonesty. They're as thick as thieves.

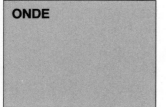

être sur la même longueur d'ondes (coll.)

to be on the same wavelength (coll.)

Bien qu'il y ait une grande différence d'âge, nous nous entendons très bien. Nous sommes sur la même longueur d'ondes.
Although there's a great difference in our ages, we get along really well. We're on the same wavelength.

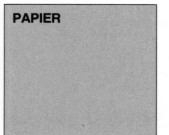

être dans les bons/petits papiers de

to get on someone's good side

Giles a fait la vaisselle pendant toute la semaine pour être dans les bons/petits papiers de ses parents. Il espérait qu'ils le laisseraient sortir le quatorze juillet jusqu'à minuit avec ses copains.
Giles washed the dishes all week to get on his parent's good side. He hoped that they would let him go out with his friends until midnight on the fourteenth of July.

A tes souhaits!

God bless you! Gesundheit!

A tes souhaits! Tu devrais prendre quelque chose pour ce rhume.
Gesundheit! You ought to take something for that cold.

39. HELP, SUPPORT, ASSISTANCE

COUDE

se serrer les coudes (coll.)

to back one another up, to stick together (coll.)

Quels que soient les problèmes que leur pose le reste du monde, les habitants de cette île se serrent toujours les coudes.
Whatever problems they come up against from the outside world, the inhabitants of this island always stick together.

COUP

donner un coup de main

to lend a hand

Pouvez-vous me donner un coup de main? Je n'arrive pas à mettre cette valise dans le filet à bagages.
Could you lend me a hand? I can't get this bag into the luggage rack.

ÉCHELLE

faire la courte échelle à quelqu'un

to give someone a boost

Si tu me fais la courte échelle, je pourrai grimper sur le toit du garage pour aller chercher le ballon.
If you give me a boost, I'll be able to climb onto the garage roof and get the ball down.

FLEUR

faire une fleur à quelqu'un (coll.)

to do someone a favor

Le garagiste nous a fait une fleur en montant, gratuitement, un auto-radio dans notre nouvelle Renault.
The garage owner did us a favor by installing a car radio in our new Renault for nothing.

METTRE

y mettre du sien

to pull one's weight

Si tu y mets du tien, nous devrons finir la construction de notre voilier en un mois.
If you pull your weight, we should finish building our sailing boat within one month.

SERRER

se serrer

to squeeze in

Pourriez-vous vous serrer s'il vous plaît pour faire de la place pour une autre personne?
Would you please squeeze in to make room for another person?

40. HOLIDAYS

ANGLAIS

filer à l'anglaise

to go AWOL (coll.), *to take an unscheduled day off*

Comme tant de personnes filaient à l'anglaise le Jour de l'An en Grande Bretagne, on a fini par en faire un jour de congé.
Because so many people took an unscheduled day off on New Year's Day in England, it was eventually declared an official national holiday.

Origin: **From a custom whereby a guest left a social gathering without saying goodbye to one's host. The French and the English each claimed that the other had originated the custom.**

Another explanation traces this idiom back to the period of the lengthy wars between the English and the French. Captives on both sides would try to escape, giving the rise to the expression "filer à l'anglaise" among the French and "to take French leave" (i.e., leave of the French) among the English combatants.

PONT

un pont

a long weekend

Pour le pont du premier mai, nous comptons aller en Auvergne. Quatre jours de repos, ça fera du bien.
For the long May Day weekend, we intend to go to Auvergne. Four days' rest will do us good.

Origin: **From the practice of taking a day off between a weekend and a public holiday as an extra day's holiday, thereby using it as a bridge ("un pont") between the official holidays.**

41. HUMOR, LAUGHTER, FUN

BARBE

rire dans sa barbe

to laugh up one's sleeve

Ce vendeur de voiture doit rire dans sa barbe. La voiture qu'il leur a vendue est vieux clou.
That car dealer must be laughing up his sleeve. The car he sold them is a lemon.

CÔTE

se tenir les côtes de rire

to split one's sides with laughter

Nous nous sommes tenu les côtes de rire quand nous avons vu les photos de papa quand il était jeune. La mode d'alors était incroyable.
We split our sides with laughter when we saw photographs of Dad in his youth. The fashions of the day were unbelievable.

GORGE

rire à gorge déployée

to roar with laughter

Les élèves ont ri à gorge déployée quand ils ont vu les efforts maladroits de leur professeur sur ses skis.
The students roared with laughter when they saw their teacher's clumsy efforts on skis.

HISTOIRE

histoire de rire

just for fun, for a laugh

Histoire de rire, racontons-lui qu'il a gagné le gros lot à la Loterie Nationale.
Just for fun, let's tell him he won the Lottery.

MARCHER

faire marcher quelqu'un

to pull someone's leg

Moi, j'ai gagné le premier prix? Tu me fais marcher, n'est-ce pas?
I've won the first prize? You're pulling my leg, aren't you?

POISSON

poisson d'avril

April fool

Le premier avril les jeunes Français aiment coller de petits poissons en papier dans le dos des adultes, et leur dire "Poisson d'avril!"
On April 1st, young French people like to stick little paper fishes on adults' backs and to say to them "April fool!"

RIRE

avoir/prendre le fou rire

to laugh uncontrollably

Nos enfants ont beaucoup aimé le cirque. Ils ont pris le fou rire pendant le numéro des clowns.
Our children loved the circus. They laughed uncontrollably during the clown's act.

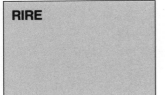

RIRE

avoir toujours le mot pour rire

to be a born joker, to be always ready for a laugh

Léon a toujours le mot pour rire. Même dans les situations difficiles sa vivacité d'esprit surprend tout le monde.
Leon is a born joker. Even in unpleasant situations his wit surprises everyone.

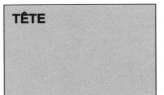

TÊTE

se payer la tête de quelqu'un (coll.)

to make fun of someone

On se payait sa tête à l'école, mais à présent elle est célèbre et riche, et tout le monde l'envie.
They used to make fun of her at school, but now she's rich and famous and the envy of them all.

42. INCREDULITY, DISBELIEF

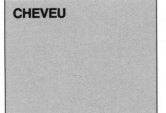

CHEVEU

tiré par les cheveux

farfetched

Jean-Luc raconte à tout le monde qu'il est descendu du sommet du Mont Blanc en delta-plane. Cela me paraît plutôt tiré par les cheveux.
Jean-Luc is telling everybody that he has been hang-gliding from the summit of Mont Blanc. That seems pretty farfetched to me.

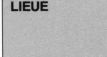

LIEUE

J'étais à mille lieues de penser que

I would never have dreamed that,
It would never have entered my mind that

J'étais à mille lieues de penser que ce vieux tableau dans mon grenier valait une fortune.
I would never have dreamed that the old painting in my attic was worth a fortune.

ŒIL

Mon œil!

My foot!

Il dit qu'il a fait l'ascension du Mont Blanc? Mon œil! Il n'est même pas capable de monter à une échelle sans avoir le vertige.
He claims he's climbed Mont Blanc? My foot! He can't even go up a ladder without getting dizzy.

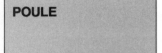

POULE

Oui, quand les poules auront des dents.

That'll be the day.

"Un de ces jours je t'offrirai un collier tout en or."
"Oui, quand les poules auront des dents."
"One of these days I'll buy you a gold necklace."
"That'll be the day."

POULE

Oui, quand les poules porteront les œufs au marché.

That'll be the day.

Quoi, te prêter ma voiture? Oui, quand les poules porteront les œufs au marché.
What, me lend you my car? That'll be the day.

43. INDECISION, INDECISIVENESS

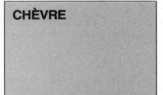

CHÈVRE

ménager la chèvre et le chou

to sit on the fence

Le jeune Député a choisi de ménager la chèvre et le chou et il s'est abstenu lors du vote.
The young Congressman chose to sit on the fence and he abstained in the vote.

Origin: **The goat and the cabbage here represent opposite poles, namely the devourer and the devoured.**

POT

tourner autour du pot

to beat around the bush

A quoi bon tourner autour du pot? J'aime autant te dire tout net que Michelle ne veut plus sortir avec toi.
There's no point in beating around the bush. I might as well tell you right out that Michelle doesn't want to go out with you anymore.

44. LISTENING, ATTENTION

MOUCHE

On aurait entendu voler une mouche.

You could have heard a pin drop.

Quand le directeur est entré dans la classe le chahut s'est arrêté et tous les élèves se sont mis debout derrière leur chaise. On aurait entendu voler une mouche.
When the principal came into the classroom the noise stopped and all the students stood behind their chairs. You could have heard a pin drop.

OREILLE	**n'écouter que d'une oreille** *to half-listen, to listen with only one ear* Comment peux-tu espérer apprendre quoi que ce soit si tu n'écoutes que d'une oreille en classe? *How can you expect to learn anything if you only half-listen in class.*

OREILLE	**faire la sourde oreille** *to turn a deaf ear* Chaque fois que je lui demande de l'argent, ma sœur me fait la sourde oreille. *Each time I ask her for money, my sister turns a deaf ear.*

■ 45. LUCK ■

BOL POT	**avoir du bol** (coll.) **avoir du pot** (coll.) *to be in luck, to be lucky* Tu as du bol/pot de pouvoir aller à ton travail à pied. On doit tous faire des trajets de plusieurs kilomètres. *You're very lucky being able to walk to work. We all have to commute several miles.*

BONHEUR	**au petit bonheur la chance** (coll.) *haphazardly, at random* Je t'avais pourtant dit de consulter la carte au dernier croisement au lieu de prendre une route au petit bonheur la chance. A présent nous sommes complètement perdus! *You see, I told you to look at the map at the last intersection instead of choosing a road at random. Now we're completely lost!*

MALHEUR	**jouer de malheur** *to have a streak of bad luck* Je joue de malheur. Ce matin j'ai manqué mon train, perdu mon portefeuille et je me suis cassé une cheville. Demain ne peut être que meilleur. *I'm having a streak of bad luck. This morning I missed my train, lost my wallet and broke my ankle. Things can only be better tomorrow.*

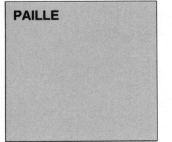

PAILLE

tirer à la courte paille

to draw straws

Puisque vous n'arrivez pas à décider lequel d'entre vous sera le porte-parole, nous devrons tirer à la courte paille.
Since you can't make up your minds about which of you will be the spokesman, we'll have to draw straws.

Origin: **From the practice of drawing straws as a way of making decisions. The person who drew the shortest straw would be the one picked to do something.**

■ 46. MISHAPS ■

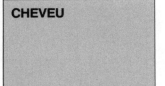

CHEVEU

tomber comme un cheveu dans la soupe

to come at the worst possible moment

Ton histoire belge est tombée comme un cheveu dans la soupe. L'invité d'honneur était Belge!
Your "Belgian" joke came at the worst possible moment. The guest of honor was Belgian!

N.B. A Belgian joke is the French equivalent of a Polish joke.

FER

tomber les quatre fers en air

to go feet forward

Le pauvre! Il n'a pas vu la peau de banane et il est tombé les quatre fers en l'air.
The poor fellow! He didn't see the banana skin and he went feet forward.

Origin: **The reference is to a horse falling on its back with its four iron horseshoes in the air.**

PELLE

prendre une pelle (coll.)

to fall flat on one's face

Le manche de sa raquette s'est pris dans les rayons de sa roue arrière et c'est comme cela que Nicolas a pris une pelle.
The handle of his racket got caught in the spokes of his back wheel and that's how Nicolas fell flat on his face.

TASSE

boire la tasse (coll.)

to swallow a mouthful (when swimming)

Quand elle m'a poussé sous l'eau, j'ai bu la tasse et je toussais tellement que j'ai dû sortir de la piscine.
When she pushed me under the water, I swallowed a mouthful and coughed so much that I had to get out of the pool.

47. MONEY

BEURRE

Cela mettra du beurre dans les épinards.

That will make life a little easier.

J'ai appris que tu as eu de l'avancement. Cela mettra du beurre dans les épinards.
I hear you've had a promotion. That will make life a little easier.

**BOUCHÉE
TROIS**

**pour une bouchée de pain
pour trois fois rien**

for next to nothing, for peanuts (coll.), for a song

Les ventes de charité sont toujours très populaires parce que l'on peut acheter des choses intéressantes pour une bouchée de pain/trois fois rien.
Rummage sales are always popular because people can buy interesting things for next to nothing.

BOUT

joindre les deux bouts

to make ends meet

Quatre enfants, toi au chômage . . . Comment joindre les deux bouts avec si peu d'argent?
Four children and you unemployed . . . How can we make ends meet on so little money?

COU

endetté jusqu'au cou

up to one's ears in debt (coll.)

Nos voisins ont acheté trop de choses à crédit. A présent ils sont endettés jusqu'au cou.
Our neighbors have bought too many things on credit. Now they're up to their ears in debt.

FAUCHÉ

fauché comme les blés

flat broke (coll.)

Cette année je ne peux pas me payer de vacances. Je suis fauché comme les blés.
I can't afford a vacation this year. I'm flat broke.

FLÈCHE

monter en flèche

to soar, to shoot up (of prices)

Depuis six mois le prix de l'essence monte en flèche.
For six months the price of gas has been shooting up.

Origin: **The picture here is that of an arrow ("une flèche") being fired into the air.**

LIQUIDE

être à court de liquide

to be short of cash

Nous sommes à court de liquide. Il va me falloir toucher un chèque.
We're short of cash. I'll have to go and cash a check.

NOTE

La note est plutôt salée. (coll.)

That's pretty steep. (coll.)

Trois cents francs pour ça! La note est plutôt salée.
Three hundred francs for that! That's pretty steep.

ŒIL

coûter les yeux de la tête

to cost an arm and a leg (coll.), *to cost a fortune*

Cela va nous coûter les yeux de la tête d'aller voir notre famille en Australie mais qu'importe l'argent? Ce sera merveilleux de les revoir.
It will cost a fortune to visit our family in Australia, but what does money matter? It will be marvelous to see them again.

PAILLE

être sur la paille

to be desperately poor, to be destitute

Les œuvres de charité s'occupent de ceux qui sont sur la paille.
Charitable organizations look after those people who are desperately poor.

POIRE

couper la poire en deux

to split the difference

Le prix que vous demandez pour votre voiture est trop élevé et vous dites que le mien est trop bas. Pourquoi ne coupons-nous pas la poire en deux?
The price you are asking for your car is too high, and you say my offer is too low. Why don't we split the difference?

PRIX

faire un prix d'ami à quelqu'un

to knock a bit off for someone (coll.), *to let someone have something cheap*

Si vous vous décidez avant demain, je vous ferai un prix d'ami — 450 francs au lieu de 500 francs.
If you make up your mind before tomorrow, I'll knock a bit off for you — 450 instead of 500 francs.

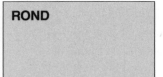

Il n'a pas un rond. (coll.)

He's broke. (coll.)

Ne demande pas à Serge de te prêter de l'argent. Il n'a pas un rond.
Don't ask Serge for a loan. He's broke.

être sans le sou

to be penniless

Sa passion pour les jeux d'argent l'a ruiné. Autrefois c'était un homme d'affaires très riche, mais à présent il est sans le sou.
His gambling has been the ruin of him. He was once a very wealthy businessman, now he's penniless.

48. MOODS

MOUCHE

Quelle mouche t'a piqué?

What's come over you?

Quelle mouche t'a piqué? Hier tu étais enchanté de ta nouvelle voiture, mais tout à coup tu veux t'en débarrasser.
What's come over you? You were perfectly happy with your new car yesterday, but all of a sudden you want to get rid of it.

PIED

se lever du pied gauche

to get up on the wrong side of the bed (coll.)

Évite-le ce matin, il est de mauvaise humeur. Il a dû se lever du pied gauche.
Avoid him this morning, he's in a bad mood. He must have gotten up on the wrong side of the bed.

POIL

être de mauvais poil (coll.)

to be in a bad mood

Elle est de mauvais poil ce matin, ménagez-la. Peut-être est-elle fatiguée?
She's in a bad mood this morning; humor her. Perhaps she's tired?

49. NATURE, OUTDOORS

BÊTE

une bête à bon Dieu

a ladybug

Nos deux enfants adorent laisser les bêtes à bon Dieu grimper le long de leurs bras.
Our two children love to let ladybugs crawl up their arms.

ÉTOILE

coucher à la belle étoile

to sleep in the open air

J'aurais bien couché à la belle étoile quand j'ai fait de l'auto-stop dans le Val de Loire, mais il a fait trop froid.
I would have liked to sleep in the open air while I was hitchhiking in the Loire Valley, but it was too cold.

FEU

un feu d'artifice

a fireworks display

En France on n'a pas de feux d'artifice le quatre juillet mais pour le jour de la Bastille.
In France they don't have fireworks displays on the Fourth of July but on Bastille Day.

50. NEWSPAPERS

CANARD

un canard (coll.)

a scandal sheet (i.e., a newspaper)

Je vois que tu as encore ta photo dans le canard.
I see you've got your picture in the local scandal sheet.

Origin: **"Un canard" was originally a sensational, often untrue, piece of news and in time it came to mean a newspaper of little standing because it printed such news.**

UNE

à la une

on the front page

A la une de tous les journaux on pouvait lire: "Le Président est mort!"
On the front page of every newspaper you could read: "The President is dead!"

51. OBVIOUSNESS

ALLER

Cela va de soi.

It goes without saying. It stands to reason.

Cela va de soi: de continuelles réductions des dépenses publiques rendront un gouvernement impopulaire auprès de beaucoup de gens.
It goes without saying: continual cuts in public spending will make a government unpopular with many people.

FIL

cousu de fil blanc

blatant, too obvious to fool anyone

Votre histoire est cousue de fil blanc. Comment espérez-vous que les gens vous croient?
Your story is too obvious to fool anyone. How do you expect people to believe you?

NEZ

au nez et à la barbe de quelqu'un

right under someone's nose

On l'a emmené à la gendarmerie parce qu'il a volé de l'argent dans la caisse au nez et à la barbe de son patron.
He was taken to the police station because he stole money from the cash register under the boss's nose.

ŒIL

Cela crève les yeux.

It's staring you in the face. It's as plain as the nose on your face.

Que veux-tu dire tu ne le savais pas? Mais cela crève les yeux: il t'adore!
What do you mean you didn't know? But it's staring you in the face: he's madly in love with you!

ŒIL

Cela saute aux yeux.

It's obvious.

Cela saute aux yeux qu'elle ne s'habille pas chez un grand couturier. Ses robes tombent toujours mal.
It's obvious that she doesn't buy clothes from a top designer. Her dresses never hang right.

TOUJOURS

toujours est-il que

the fact remains

Toujours est-il que, malgré son âge, il reste un joueur exceptionnel. Je ne comprends pas pourquoi il n'est plus dans l'équipe nationale.
The fact remains that, in spite of his age, he's still an exceptional player. I don't understand why he's no longer on the national team.

52. OCCUPATIONS

DRAPEAU

être sous les drapeaux

to be in the armed forces, to be in the service

Notre fils aîné est sous les drapeaux depuis août. Il est dans un régiment parachutiste.
Our eldest son has been in the service since August. He's in a parachute regiment.

PLANCHE

monter sur les planches

to go on the stage

C'est à l'âge de quinze ans qu'il est monté sur les planches pour la première fois. Ce devait être le début d'une remarquable carrière théâtrale.
He was fifteen when he first went on the stage. It was to be the start of a remarkable theatrical career.

RAYON

C'est son rayon.

That's his line. (coll.) That's his specialty.

L'électronique, c'est son rayon. Si tu as un problème, c'est à lui que tu dois t'adresser.
Electronics is his line. If you have a problem, he's the one to go to.

Origin: **"Un rayon" is a department in a large store. The person in charge of such a department is assumed to be knowledgeable about it and competent to run it.**

53. OUTCOME, RESULT

CAROTTE

Ses carottes sont cuites! (coll.)

He's done for! (coll.) He's had it! (coll.)

Ton père sait que tu as volé ce vélo. Tes carottes sont cuites.
Your father knows you stole that bike. You've had it.

CHANDELLE

en voir trente-six chandelles

to see stars

La première fois que j'ai essayé de skier je n'ai pas pu m'arrêter et j'ai heurté un arbre. J'en ai vu trente-six chandelles.
At my first attempt at skiing I couldn't stop and bumped into a tree. I saw stars.

Origin: **Prior to the advent of electricity, candles were extremely important as a source of light. In this idiom the use of "chandelle" is synonymous with light, "trente-six" emphasizing the degree of "light" that one might experience after a blow to the head.**

CHEVAL

un remède de cheval

a drastic remedy, drastic measures

Le gouvernement a prescrit un remède de cheval cette fois-ci pour freiner l'inflation. Etait-ce vraiment nécessaire?
The government has prescribed a drastic remedy this time to curb inflation. Was it really necessary?

CINQ

Il était moins cinq.

It was a close shave/a narrow squeak (coll.)/*a close call.*

On a failli écraser un chat qui s'était échappé dans la rue. Il était moins cinq.
We just missed hitting a cat that had run into the street. It was a close call.

Origin: **From the time. The full hour is almost up.**

ÉCHAPPER

l'échapper belle

to have a narrow escape

Sa voiture est restée suspendue au-dessus du précipice. Il l'a échappé belle.
His car stayed suspended over the precipice. He had a narrow escape.

ÉPONGE

passer l'éponge

to forget it

Bon, c'est parfait. Tu as fait tes excuses, à présent passons l'éponge.
OK, that's fine. You've apologized. Now let's forget it.

FOUET

de plein fouet

head-on

Les deux voitures se sont heurtées de plein fouet et il n'y a eu aucun survivant.
The two cars collided head-on and there were no survivors.

GOUTTE

C'est la goutte d'eau qui fait déborder le vase.

It's the straw that broke the camel's back. That's the last straw.

Leurs conditions de travail se sont détériorées et à présent on leur refuse une augmentation. C'est la goutte d'eau qui va faire déborder le vase.
Their conditions at work have been getting worse and now they've been refused a pay raise. That's the last straw.

MAL

tomber dans les pommes/se trouver mal

to faint, to pass out (coll.)

Il faisait chaud et on manquait d'air dans le stade bondé de gens. Pas étonnant que tant de personnes soient tombées dans les pommes.
It was hot and stuffy in the crowded stadium. Little wonder that many people fainted.

Origin: **Nothing to do with apples. "Pommes" here derives from "paumez" which in turn became "pasme," then "pame" meaning "in a swoon." In Normandy the word "paume" (from "paumez") is still used.**

PARLER

trouver à qui parler

to meet one's match

Le champion d'échecs a fini par trouver à qui parler; un jeune prodige vient de le battre trois fois de suite.
The chess champion has finally met his match; a young prodigy has beaten him three times in a row.

PIPE

casser sa pipe (coll.)

to kick the bucket (coll.)

Le vieux Yves a cassé sa pipe. Il avait presque cent ans.
Old Yves has kicked the bucket. He was nearly a hundred.

POISSON

finir en queue de poisson

to end abruptly, to leave someone hanging (coll.)

Quel dommage! Le début de ton histoire était excellent, mais elle a fini en queue de poisson.
What a pity! Your story had an excellent beginning, but it left me hanging.

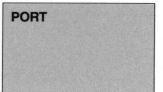

arriver à bon port

to arrive safely

Quel long voyage — 1.300 kilomètres en deux jours! Nous voici enfin arrivés à bon port.
What a long trip — 1,300 kilometers in two days! At last we've arrived safely.

payer les pots cassés

to pay for the damage

C'est typique! Encore une fois c'est Marcel qui a causé tous ces ennuis et c'est quelqu'un d'autre qui doit payer les pots cassés.

It's typical of Marcel! Once again he's caused the trouble and someone else has had to pay for the damage.

54. PRACTICE

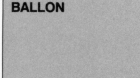

un ballon d'essai

a trial run

Le fabricant a décidé qu'il serait prudent de faire un ballon d'essai pour voir si le public aimerait un dentifrice au citron.
The manufacturer decided that it would be prudent to have a trial run to see if the public would like a lemon-flavored toothpaste.

une mise en train

a warm-up

Après une brève mise en train les joueurs de tennis ont commencé leur match.
After a short warm-up the tennis players began their match.

55. PUNISHMENT

coller (coll.)

to keep someone in (school)

C'est la première fois que j'ai oublié de faire mes devoirs de maths, et bien il m'a quand même collé.
It's the first time I forgot to do my math homework, but even so he still kept me in.

FAIRE

C'est bien fait pour toi.

It serves you right.

Quoi! Ton cerf-volant est coincé dans l'arbre? C'est bien fait pour toi. On t'avait bien dit de ne pas jouer là.
What! Your kite got stuck in the tree? It serves you right. We told you not to play there.

OMBRE

mettre quelqu'un à l'ombre (coll.)

to put someone behind bars (coll.)

La police a fini par l'attraper après deux ans de recherches, et on l'a mis à l'ombre.
The police finally caught him after a two-year investigation, and put him behind bars.

PIED

mettre à pied

to dismiss, to fire

On vient de le mettre à pied. Ce n'est pas surprenant, il ne faisait strictement rien.
He's just been fired. It's not surprising, he did no work at all.

SALER

saler (coll.)

to be tough on (coll.)

Le juge l'a vraiment salé: dix ans de prison!
The judge was really tough on him: ten years in prison!

VIS

serrer la vis à quelqu'un (coll.)

to crack down on someone (coll.), *to put the screws on someone* (coll.)

Ses parents devraient lui serrer la vis. A quatorze ans il a beaucoup trop de liberté.
His parents ought to crack down on him. At fourteen he has far too much freedom.

56. QUANTITY, AMOUNT, NUMBER

CHAMP

à tout bout de champ

forever, at every turn

A tout bout de champ il parle de ses opérations et de ses maladies. A croire qu'il n'a aucun autre sujet de conversation.
He's forever talking about his operations and his illnesses. You'd think he had no other topic of conversation.

CHAT

Il n'y avait pas un chat.

There wasn't a soul.

Il faisait une telle canicule hier après-midi qu'il n'y avait pas un chat en ville. Tous les gens avaient dû rester chez eux.
There was such a heat wave yesterday afternoon that there wasn't a soul in town. Everyone must have stayed indoors.

CORPS

corps et biens

with all hands on board

Au début on a cru qu'il y aurait des survivants, mais la police vient de confirmer que le navire a été perdu corps et biens.
At first it was thought that there would be some survivors, but the police have just confirmed that the ship was lost with all hands on board.

DOIGT

un doigt de

a drop of

Vous prendrez bien un doigt de cognac, n'est-ce pas?
You will have a drop of brandy, won't you?

FOU

plus on est de fous, plus on rit

the more, the merrier

Bien sûr, Pascal peut venir à notre soirée. Plus on est de fous, plus on rit.
Of course, Pascal can come to our party. The more, the merrier.

GOGO

à gogo (coll.)

in abundance, galore, to burn (coll.)

Depuis son avancement on sent qu'il a de l'argent à gogo. En moins d'un an il s'est payé des vacances en Grèce, une Porsche et un mois à Chamonix.
Since his promotion you can tell he has money to burn. In less than a year he has treated himself to a vacation in Greece, a Porsche, and one month in Chamonix.

Origin: **From "gogue" meaning "amusement," "entertainment." "Être dans les gogues" meant "to be joyful." By extension, the word came to imply abundance (of joy, etc).**

MAL

pas mal de gens

quite a few people

Malgré le mauvais temps, il y avait pas mal de gens à la kermesse.
Despite the bad weather, there were quite a few people at the fair.

MONDE

un monde fou (coll.)

a huge crowd

Il y avait un monde fou pour accueillir la vedette de cinéma à l'aéroport.
There was a huge crowd to welcome the movie star at the airport.

MONDE

Il n'y a pas grand monde.

There aren't many people.

"Il n'y a pas grand monde en ville aujourd'hui,"
"Je pense que c'est à cause de ce virus."
"There aren't many people in town today."
"I suppose it's because of the virus that's going around."

PELÉ

Il n'y avait que trois pelés et un tondu.

There was hardly anybody there.

Leur kermesse n'a pas eu de succès cette année. Il n'y avait que trois pelés et un tondu.
Their charity fair was not a success this year. There was hardly anyone there.

57. RATE, PROGRESSION

AIGUILLE

de fil en aiguille

gradually, little by little

Il a commencé par vendre des vêtements sur les marchés, mais de fil en aiguille il a agrandi son entreprise et, à présent, il est propriétaire d'une chaîne de grands magasins.
He started off selling clothes at open-air markets, but gradually he built up his business and now he owns a chain of department stores.

COUP

coup sur coup

in close succession, one after another

Coup sur coup trois des members du Cabinet ont démissionné.
One after another, three members of the Cabinet resigned.

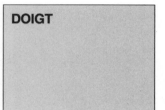

mettre le doigt dans l'engrenage

to become involved in something

Attention! Une fois que vous aurez mis le doigt dans l'engrenage, impossible de faire demi-tour. Le crime ne paie pas.
Watch out! Once you've become involved, it will be impossible to turn back. Crime doesn't pay.

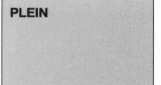

faire tache d'huile
faire boule de neige

to gain ground, to gather momentum, to snowball

L'idée d'un concert de charité a fait tache d'huile/boule de neige, et en quelques semaines on a recueilli plusieurs millions de francs.
The idea of a charity concert gained ground and within a few weeks millions of francs were raised.

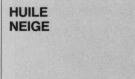

battre son plein

to be in full swing, to be in high gear

Quand nous sommes arrivés vers 3 heures, la fête battait déjà son plein.
When we arrived around 3 p.m., the party was already in full swing.

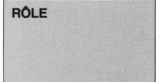

à tour de rôle

in turn

Cela ne sert à rien de pousser. Nous ne pouvons nous occuper de vos demandes de renseignements qu'à tour de rôle.
There's no point in pushing. We can only deal with your inquiries in turn.

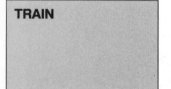

au train où vont les choses

at this rate, at the rate things are going

Au train où vont les choses, le gouvernement devra prendre des mesures draconiennes pour juguler l'inflation.
At the rate things are going, the government will have to take drastic measures to stop inflation.

58. REPROACHES

CLOCHE

se faire sonner les cloches par quelqu'un

to be read the riot act by someone

J'avais oublié de fermer le robinet. Je me suis fait sonner les cloches par mon père.
I had forgotten to turn off the faucet. My father read me the riot act.

SAVON

passer un savon à quelqu'un (coll.)

to rake someone over the coals, to come down hard on someone (coll.)

C'est la troisième fois qu'il est en retard cette semaine. Quel savon le patron va lui passer!
It's the third time he's been late this week. The boss is going to rake him over the coals!

Origin: **From "savonner la tête," which came to indicate an energetic way of cleaning someone's head, and hence, by extension, to rebuke someone.**

59. RECREATION

BOÎTE

une boîte de nuit

a nightclub

Qu'est-ce qu'ils font ce soir? Cinéma? Disco? Ou boîte de nuit? Ils ne restent jamais chez eux.
What are they doing this evening? Movies? Disco? Or nightclub? They never stay in.

CHAMPAGNE

sabler le champagne

to drink champagne

On a sablé le champagne pour fêter sa victoire aux élections.
They drank champagne to celebrate his victory in the elections.

Origin: **The traditional explanation is that bubbling wine conjures up a picture of molten metal being poured into a sand mold. This process is called "sabler" in French.**

COULER

se la couler douce (coll.)

to take it easy

Depuis qu'il a pris sa retraite, il se la coule douce. Un peu de pêche, de petites promenades — c'est la bonne vie.
Since his retirement he's been taking it easy. A little fishing, some short walks — he's enjoying life.

LÈCHE

faire du lèche-vitrine (coll.)

to go window-shopping

Ma femme adore faire du lèche-vitrine. Personnellement je trouve cela ennuyeux comme tout.
My wife loves window-shopping. Personally I find it extremely boring.

MACHINE

une machine à sous (coll.)

one-armed bandit (coll.), *slot machine*

Quand ils prennent le bateau pour venir en Angleterre, beaucoup de jeunes Français se précipitent sur les machines à sous. Celles-ci sont interdites en France.
When they get on the boat to England, a lot of young French people rush to the one-armed bandits. They are illegal in France.

TÊTE

piquer une tête (coll.)

to dive

Il faisait si chaud que nous avons tous décidé de piquer une tête dans la rivière.
It was so hot that we all decided to dive into the river.

VIOLON

un violon d'Ingres

a hobby

Lui, son violon d'Ingres c'est la philatélie. Il passe des heures à étudier et ranger des milliers de timbres.
His hobby is stamp collecting. He spends hours studying and arranging thousands of stamps.

Origin: **From the fact that Ingres, the painter, used to play the violin in his spare time.**

60. RUMOR

BRUIT

le bruit court

rumor has it

Le bruit court qu'on va construire un nouveau complexe sportif, mais j'y croirai seulement quand je le verrai.
Rumor has it that a new sports center is going to be built here, but I'll believe it when I see it.

BRUIT

faire courir le bruit

to spread the rumor

Les élèves de sixième ont fait courir le bruit que les grandes vacances allaient commencer le premier juin.
The sixth graders spread the rumor that summer vacation was going to begin on June 1st.

61. SECRETS

MÈCHE

vendre la mèche (coll.)

to let the cat out of the bag, to give it away (a secret)

La classe allait faire une farce au professeur le premier avril, mais un de élèves a vendu la mèche et le lui a dit.
The class was going to play a trick on the teacher on April 1st but one of the students let the cat out of the bag and told him.

MOTUS

Motus et bouche cousue!

Keep it under your hat! (coll.) *Mum's the word!* (coll.)

Le Directeur prend sa retraite à la fin du trimestre mais motus et bouche cousue. Il ne veut pas que les élèves le sachent déjà.
The principal is retiring at the end of the quarter, but keep it under your hat! He doesn't want the pupils to know yet.

Origin: "Motus" is a latinization of the French "mot" used as an interjection to demand silence, i.e., "pas un mot." In this idiom "motus" is sometimes used alone, although usually with "et bouche cousue."

ŒIL

entre quatre yeux

between you and me

Entre quatre yeux, on m'a dit que c'est lui le prochain patron. Surtout ne le répétez à personne.
Between you and me, I've been told that he's going to be the new boss. Whatever you do, don't tell anyone.

62. SICKNESS, HEALTH

ASSIETTE

ne pas être dans son assiette

to be under the weather (coll.), *to be out of sorts* (coll.)

Depuis ma grippe je ne suis pas dans mon assiette. Je vais prendre un fortifiant.
Since I've had the flu I've been under the weather. I'm going to take a tonic.

Origin: **"Assiette" at one time simply referred to the position of being "assis," i.e., seated. Thus one could speak of "la bonne assiette d'un cavalier sur la selle." The term "assiette" is still used in this sense today in flying: a pilot corrects "l'assiette de son avion."**

ATTAQUE

être d'attaque (coll.)

in top form

Elle s'est bien remise de sa mauvaise grippe et à présent elle est d'attaque.
She recovered from her bad flu and now she's in top form.

BRILLANT

ne pas être très brillant

one's health isn't too good

Depuis son accident il n'est pas très brillant. Il a toujours des vertiges et des maux de tête.
Since his accident he hasn't been too good. He still gets dizzy spells and headaches.

CHARME

se porter comme un charme (coll.)

to be as fit as a fiddle

Après sa longue maladie il se porte à nouveau comme un charme.
After his long illness he's as fit as a fiddle again.

CHEVAL

une fièvre de cheval (coll.)

a raging fever

Maxine est couchée. Elle est malade et a une fièvre de cheval.
Maxine is in bed. She's sick and has a raging fever.

Origin: **"De cheval" like "de chien" is used disparagingly. The French seem to have held horses and dogs in low regard at one time.**

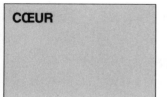**CŒUR**

avoir mal au cœur

to feel sick, to feel nauseated

La mer était très agitée et j'ai eu mal au cœur pendant toute la traversée.
The sea was very rough and I felt sick during the whole crossing.

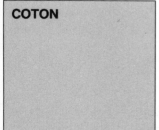**COTON**

filer du mauvais coton

to be in bad shape (health)

Il a beaucoup bu et fumé pendant des années et il file du mauvais coton. S'il ne change pas ses mauvaises habitudes tout de suite, il sera trop tard.
After years of heavy smoking and drinking, he's in bad shape. If he doesn't change his bad habits at once, it will be too late.

Origin: **Uncertain, but possibly it derives from the fact that the first coton-spinning machines in the eighteenth century were often faulty and caused production problems.**

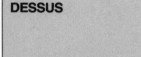**DESSUS**

reprendre le dessus

to get over (an illness), to recover

Martine a eu la grippe pendant quelques jours, mais je suis heureuse de voir qu'elle a repris le dessus.
Martine has been ill with the flu for a while, but I'm glad to say that she's over it now.

**LIT**

être cloué au lit

to be bedridden

Il est cloué au lit depuis son opération.
He's been bedridden since his operation.

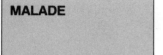**MALADE**

se faire porter malade

to call in sick

Richard ne viendra pas au bureau aujourd'hui. Il s'est fait porter malade.
Richard won't be in the office today. He's called in sick.

PIED

avoir bon pied bon œil

to be hale and hearty

Quelle santé! A quatre-vingt cinq ans elle a toujours bon pied bon œil.
What health! At 85 she is still hale and hearty.

POINT

être mal en point

to be in bad shape (health)

Ma grand-mère est mal en point depuis sa chute l'hiver dernier.
My grandmother has been in bad shape since her fall last winter.

PORTER

se porter bien

to be well (also, to be plump)

se porter mal

to be ill

Je suis heureux de voir que, après sa longue maladie, ton frère se porte bien de nouveau.
I'm pleased to see that your brother is well again after his long illness.

RADIO

la radio

X-ray

Regardez, on voit très bien à la radio que cet os est fracturé.
Look, you can easily see from the X-ray that this bone is broken.

Origin: **The abbreviation for "la radiophotographie."**

REVENIR

revenir à soi

to come around

Je me souviens de m'être cogné la tête, et puis plus rien. Quand je suis revenu à moi, j'étais dans une ambulance.
I remember banging my head, and then nothing. When I came around, I was in an ambulance.

TRAIN

se sentir mal en train

to feel out of sorts, not to feel too good (coll.)

Je crois que je vais rester au lit aujourd'hui. Je me sens mal en train.
I think I'll stay in bed today. I don't feel too good.

63. SIMILARITY

BONNET

C'est bonnet blanc et blanc bonnet.

It's exactly the same. It's one and the same.

Vous m'aviez promis plusieurs changements, mais je vois que votre nouveau projet et l'original, c'est bonnet blanc et blanc bonnet.
You promised several changes, but I see that your new project and the original one are one and the same.

ÉGAL
KIF-KIF

Cela m'est égal.
C'est kif-kif. (coll.)

It makes no difference. It's all the same.

"Quel film veux-tu regarder, celui de la première chaîne ou celui d'Antenne 2?"
"Cela m'est égal./C'est kif-kif. Je les ai déjà vus tous les deux."
"Which movie do you want to watch — the one on Channel 1, or the one on Channel 2?"
"It makes no difference. I've seen them both before."

Origin: **"Kif-kif" is from the Arabic equivalent of "comme comme" meaning "so-so."**

64. SKILLS, ABILITIES

BEAU

faire le beau

to sit up and beg (of dogs)

Ça y est! Depuis hier notre chien fait le beau, mais il faut lui donner un os d'abord.
We've done it! Since yesterday our dog can sit up and beg, but you have to give him a bone first.

DOIGT

avoir des doigts de fée

to have nimble fingers

C'est ta mère qui a fait cette robe superbe? Elle a vraiment des doigts de fée.
Did your mother make that magnificent dress? She's really got nimble fingers.

PIED

avoir le pied marin

to be a good sailor

Je n'ai pas le pied marin. Je me sens mal même dans un pédalo!
I'm not a good sailor. I even feel sick in a paddleboat!

65. SLEEP

NUIT

passer une nuit blanche

to spend a sleepless night

J'avais tellement de soucis que j'ai passé une nuit blanche, et ce matin je dormais debout.
I had so many things on my mind that I had a sleepless night and I haven't been able to keep my eyes open this morning.

Origin: **From the Romanic "blancus" meaning "white" which in both French and English developed the figurative meaning of "empty," e.g., French "nuit blanche" (a night "empty" of sleep) and English "blank check."**

ŒIL

ne dormir que d'un œil

to catch only a few winks

Je n'ai dormi que d'un œil la nuit passée. Notre fils cadet a beaucoup toussé et cela m'a tenue en éveil.
I only caught a few winks last night. Our younger son coughed a lot and that kept me awake.

ŒIL

ne pas fermer l'œil

not to sleep a wink

Hier, je n'ai pas fermé l'œil de la nuit. L'orage m'a tenu éveillé.
I couldn't sleep a wink last night. The storm kept me awake.

OREILLE

dormir sur ses deux oreilles

to sleep soundly

Ce soir, je vais pouvoir dormir sur mes deux oreilles. J'ai fini de taper le dernier chapitre de mon livre.
I'll be able to sleep soundly tonight. I've finished typing the last chapter of my book.

POING

dormir à poings fermés

to be sound asleep

Je dormais à poings fermés quand le téléphone a sonné. Je me suis réveillé en sursaut.
I was sound asleep when the phone rang. I woke up with a start.

MATINÉE

faire la grasse matinée

to sleep in, to sleep late

Qui n'adore pas faire la grasse matinée pendant les vacances? Quoi! Vous préférez vous lever tôt et faire un tour en velo?
Who doesn't love to sleep late during vacations? What! You'd rather get up early and go for a bike ride?

Origin: **Possibly from the idea that lying in bed too long in the morning will make one "gras," i.e., fat.**

Another explanation is that "gras" here derives from the Latin "crassus" meaning "thick, dense" referring to the "density" or length of one's sleep when it extends well into the morning.

66. SORROW, REGRET

BREDOUILLER

bredouiller une excuse

to mumble an apology

Quand il a bousculé la vieille dame, c'est à peine si le gamin a bredouillé une excuse.
When he bumped into the old lady, the kid barely managed to mumble an apology.

Origin: **From the Old French "bredeler" = "bretonner" meaning to speak like a Breton in an unclear fashion.**

CUIRE

en cuire

to be sorry (i.e., regret something)

Il va t'en cuire si les douaniers te demandent d'ouvrir ton coffre. Tu as beaucoup trop de vin et de cognac.
You'll be sorry if the customs officers ask you to open your trunk. You've got far too much wine and brandy.

PAYER

être payé pour le savoir

to learn things the hard way

Je suis payé pour le savoir. Je n'ai pas tenu compte des conseils de mes parents et je me suis trouvé sans diplôme et sans travail à dix-huit ans.
I learned things the hard way. I paid no attention to my parents' advice and at eighteen I found myself without any qualifications or a job.

67. SPEED

DEUX
RIEN
SEC

en moins de deux
en moins de rien
en cinq sec (coll.)

in a flash, in no time, in the twinkling of an eye

Quand elle a appris que l'on avait conduit son fils à l'hôpital, elle y était en moins de deux/rien/en cinq sec.
When she heard that her son had been taken to the hospital, she was there in a flash.

FEU

On n'y a vu que du feu.

You hardly had time to blink.

Le voleur s'est saisi du collier si adroitement et si vite que le vendeur n'y a vu que du feu.
The thief grabbed the necklace so skillfully and so quickly that the clerk hardly had time to blink.

PIED

au pied levé

at a moment's notice

Dix minutes avant le début de la pièce un des comédiens est tombé malade. Il a fallu le remplacer au pied levé.
Ten minutes before the start of the play, one of the actors became ill. He had to be replaced at a moment's notice.

PIED

d'arrache-pied

at full speed, at breakneck speed

Les maçons ont travaillé d'arrache-pied pour terminer leur chantier avant les grands froids.
The builders worked at breakneck speed to complete the project before the cold weather.

POUDRE

se répandre comme une traînée de poudre

to spread like wildfire

La nouvelle qu'ils avaient gagné cinq cent mille francs s'est répandue comme une traînée de poudre.
The news that they had won 500,000 francs spread like wildfire.

TRAIN

à fond de train

at full speed, at full tilt

Quand Auguste a vu le taureau se diriger vers lui, il a traversé le champ à fond de train dans la direction du portail.
When Auguste saw the bull coming towards him, he ran at full tilt across the field towards the gate.

VENTRE

aller/courir ventre à terre

to go/run at top speed (coll.)

Nous avons couru ventre à terre pour prendre le dernier train, mais nous l'avons quand même manqué.
We ran at top speed to catch the last train, but we missed it.

68. STUPIDITY, INCOMPETENCE

ARAIGNÉE

avoir une araignée au plafond (coll.)

to have a screw loose (coll.)

Oui, je sais, c'est un comique, mais pour raconter autant de blagues risquées il doit avoir une araignée au plafond. Cela va nuire à sa réputation.
Yes, I know, he's a comedian, but he must have a screw loose to tell so many risqué jokes. It will hurt his reputation.

BÊTE

être bête comme ses pieds (coll.)

to be bonkers (coll.), *to be too stupid for words*

Il est bête comme ses pieds. L'autre jour je l'ai entendu se disputer avec une cabine téléphonique.
He's bonkers. The other day I heard him arguing with a telephone booth.

BOULE

perdre la boule (coll.)

to go off one's rocker (coll.), *to go around the bend* (coll.)

Je suis persuadé que Jacques a perdu la boule. Il a abandonné ses études et a décidé de faire le tour du monde en auto-stop.
I'm convinced that Jacques has gone off his rocker. He's given up his studies and decided to hitchhike around the world.

Origin: **"La boule" is used colloquially for the head.**

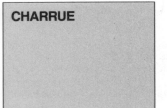

mettre la charrue devant les bœufs

to put the cart before the horse

Ne mets pas la charrue devant les bœufs. Avant de chercher à acheter une voiture, prends des leçons à une auto-école.
Don't put the cart before the horse. Before you try to buy a car, take some driving lessons.

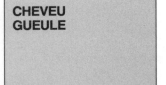

avoir mal aux cheveux (coll.)
avoir la gueule de bois (coll.)

to have a hangover

Hier soir il a trop bu et ce matin il a mal aux cheveux/la gueule de bois. Il a juré de ne plus jamais boire.
Last night he had too much to drink and this morning he's got a hangover. He swears he'll never drink again.

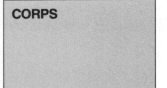

à corps perdu

recklessly

Il s'est lancé à corps perdu dans cette nouvelle aventure. Je redoute un autre échec.
He's thrown himself recklessly into this new venture. I'm afraid he'll fail again.

brûler un feu rouge

to go through a red light

Ce chauffard a brûlé un feu rouge. Il a de la chance de ne pas avoir causé d'accident.
That crazy driver went through a red light. He's lucky he didn't cause an accident.

Il n'a pas inventé le fil à couper le beurre.

He's not very bright.

Claude n'a pas inventé le fil à couper le beurre. Même quand on lui donne une liste de commissions, il ramène toujours les mauvaises provisions.
Claude is not very bright. Even when you give him a shopping list, he always brings the wrong things back.

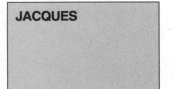

faire le Jacques (coll.)

to act like a fool

Sois sage un peu! Si tu n'arrête pas de faire le Jacques, ton père va te donner une gifle.
Just behave! If you don't stop acting like a fool, your father will smack you.

JEU

faire le jeu de quelqu'un

to play into someone's hands

Tu as fait son jeu quand tu as dit à l'antiquaire que c'était exactement le bureau que tu cherchais. Pas étonnant que tu aies dû le payer si cher.
You played into the antique dealer's hands when you told him that was the desk you were looking for. No wonder you had to pay so much for it.

MANQUER

Il n'en manque jamais une. (coll.)

He blunders every time. (coll.) He always puts his foot in it. (coll.)

Paul n'en manque jamais une. Il a demandé à Mme Dupont des nouvelles de son mari — une semaine après leur divorce!
Paul always put his foot in it. He asked Mme. Dupont how her husband was a week after they had been divorced.

Origin: **"Une" here stands for "une bêtise," i.e., a blunder, something foolish.**

ŒUF

mettre tous ses œufs dans le même panier

to put all one's eggs in one basket

Ne mets pas tous tes œufs dans le même panier. Tu devrais investir ton argent dans deux ou trois compagnies différentes au lieu d'une seule.
Don't put all your eggs in one basket. You ought to invest your money in two or three different companies instead of just one.

PANNEAU

tomber dans le panneau (coll.)

to fall for it (coll.), to walk right into it (coll.)

Pour rire, on a dit à Jules qu'on avait vu un requin dans la baie. Il est tombé dans le panneau, et il a refusé d'aller se baigner.
Just for a laugh we told Jules that a shark had been seen in the bay. He fell for it and refused to go for a swim.

Origin: **In the Middle Ages "un panneau" was a trap made of cloth or netting to catch game.**

PASSOIRE

Sa memoire est une vraie passoire.

He has a memory like a sieve.

Sa mémoire est une vraie passoire. Il a même oublié la date de sa convocation.
He has a memory like a sieve. He even forgot the date of the interview for his job.

PIED

faire quelque chose comme un pied (coll.)

not to have a clue (about how to do something) (coll.)

Voilà cinq ans qu'il a son permis de conduire, et il conduit toujours comme un pied.
He's had his driver's license for five years now and he still doesn't have a clue about driving.

PIED

mettre les pieds dans le plat

to put one's foot in it (coll.)

Tu as vraiment mis les pieds dans le plat quand tu as dit à Marie que nous lui avions acheté un nouveau vélo. Ce devait être une surprise.
You really put your foot in it when you told Marie we bought a new bike for her. It was supposed to be a surprise.

PLAT

en faire tout un plat (coll.)

to make such a fuss (coll.), *to make a big to-do* (coll.)

N'en faites pas tout un plat. Après tout, ce n'est qu'une petite éraflure.
Don't make such a fuss. It's only a litle scratch, after all.

QUEUE

n'avoir ni queue ni tête

to make no sense

Je regrette, mon vieux, mais ton histoire n'a ni queue ni tête. Comment veux-tu qu'on te croie?
I'm sorry, pal, but your story doesn't make sense. How do you expect people to believe you?

TÊTE

Où as-tu la tête?

What are you thinking of?

Où as-tu la tête? Tu as mis une chaussette noire et une verte!
What are you thinking of? You've put on one black sock and one green!

VACHE

parler français comme une vache espagnole

to murder French (coll.)

John est installé en France depuis six ans, mais il continue à parler français comme une vache espagnole.
John has been living in France for six years, but he continues to murder French.

VERRE

avoir un verre dans le nez (coll.)

to have one too many (coll.)

C'est souvent qu'il a un verre dans le nez. Il boit vraiment trop.
He often has one too many. He really drinks too much.

69. SUCCESS

AVOIR

Il n'y en a eu que pour quelqu'un.

to steal the show

Le jeune joueur de tennis non-classé a été brillant dans son match contre le favori. Il n'y en a eu que pour lui.
The young unseeded tennis player was brilliant in his match against the favorite. He stole the show.

BONHOMME

faire son petit bonhomme de chemin

to do quite nicely (coll.)

Le voici sous-directeur et cela en moins de cinq ans. Il a fait son petit bonhomme de chemin.
Here he is, assistant director, and all in less than five years. He's done quite nicely.

BRAS

avoir le bras long

to be influential, to have clout

Demande à Monsieur le Maire de t'aider à trouver un appartement. Il a le bras long.
Ask the mayor to help you get an apartment. He's got clout.

ÊTRE

Ça y est!

That's it!

Ça y est, j'ai compris! Il suffit de relâcher l'embrayage et d'accélérer en même temps.
That's it. I've got it! All you have to do is let go of the clutch and accelerate at the same time.

HEURE

A la bonne heure!

Good for you! Way to go! (coll.)

Tu vas commencer les révisions pour ton examen? A la bonne heure!
You're going to start reviewing for your test? Good for you!

MILLE

mettre dans le mille/être en plein dans le mille

to be right on target (coll.), *to be right on* (coll.)

Tu as mis dans le mille. Elle a quarante ans.
You're right on target. She's forty.

MONDE

avoir le monde à ses pieds

to have the world at one's feet

Riche, célèbre, une très belle femme — il avait le monde à ses pieds. Puis il s'est mis à boire, et a fini par tout perdre.
Rich, famous, a very beautiful wife — he had the world at his feet. Then he began to drink and ended up losing everything.

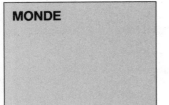

MOUCHE

faire mouche

to hit home, to score

Tu as vraiment fait mouche quand tu as dit à Sylvie qu'elle était vaniteuse, mais je doute qu'elle veuille te reparler un jour.
You really hit home when you told Sylvie that she's conceited, but I doubt if she will ever speak to you again.

Origin: **As weapons became more accurate, targets in competitions had to be refined. Hence the white center of the familiar bull's-eye had a small black patch inserted into it that was similar to the "mouche galante" (beauty spot) that ladies used to stick on their cheeks. This black patch became the new bull's-eye and was referred to as "la mouche."**

PAIN

se vendre comme des petits pains

to sell like hot cakes

Bien qu'elle soit à présent très âgée, ses disques continuent à se vendre comme des petits pains. Sa popularité semble éternelle.
Although she is now quite old, her records still sell like hot cakes. Her popularity seems to be timeless.

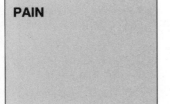

PIERRE

faire d'une pierre deux coups

to kill two birds with one stone.

Au supermarché nous avons fait d'une pierre deux coups. Nous avons fait les courses de la semaine, et aussi acheté des chaussures pour les enfants.
We killed two birds with one stone at the supermarket. We did the weekly shopping and bought shoes for the children.

POCHE

C'est dans la poche! (coll.)

It's in the bag! (coll.)

C'est dans la poche! Ils ont accepté mon offre, et demain nous signons le contrat.
It's in the bag! They've accepted my offer and tomorrow we're signing the contract.

ROULETTE

marcher comme sur des roulettes (coll.)

to go like clockwork, to go without a hitch (coll.)

Le déménagement a marché comme sur des roulettes. Rien n'a été cassé et nous n'avons mis que deux heures.
The move went like clockwork. Nothing was broken and we were finished in only two hours!

VENT

avoir le vent en poupe

to have the wind in one's sails

D'après les derniers sondages ils ont le vent en poupe et devraient remporter les élections.
According to the latest opinion polls they've got the wind in their sails and they should win the election.

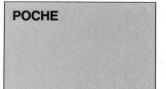

■■■■ 70. SUMMATION, CONCLUSION, ■■■■ FINALITY

CROIX

faire une croix sur quelque chose

to give something up for good

Mon père fumait beaucoup, mais quand le médecin lui a montré une radio de ses poumons, il a fait une croix sur les cigarettes.
My father used to smoke heavily, but when the doctor showed him an X-ray of his lungs, he gave up cigarettes for good.

MALHEUR

pour comble de malheur

on top of all that, to top it all off

La voiture est tombée en panne, il pleut à verse et pour comble de malheur, je suis perdu. Quelle journée!
The car has broken down, it's pouring rain and to top it all off, I'm lost. What a day!

MARCHÉ

par dessus le marché

on top of all that

Non seulement quelqu'un a-t-il volé mon argent, mais par dessus le marché j'ai perdu mon passeport. Quelles vacances!
Not only did someone steal my money, but on top of all that I lost my passport. What a vacation!

POINT

faire le point

to take stock

Bien, à présent faisons le point. Où en êtes-vous des répétitions? Les décors sont prêts?
Right, let's take stock now. How far have you gotten with the rehearsals? Is the scenery ready?

SOMME

somme toute

when all is said and done, after all

En dépit de la qualité du travail, les meubles de cette pièce ne sont, somme toute, qu'une imitation de meubles d'époque.
In spite of the quality of the craftmanship, the furniture in this room is, after all, only a period imitation.

SOMME

en somme

all in all

Vous jouez très mal du piano. En somme, toutes mes leçons ont été une pure perte de temps.
You play the piano very badly. All in all, my lessons have been a complete waste of time.

71. SURPRISE

BOUCHE

rester bouche bée

to have one's jaw drop (in surprise)

Quand il a appris que sa grand-mère avait fait de la planche à voile, il est resté bouche bée.
When he heard that his grandmother had been wind-surfing , his jaw dropped.

BOUCHE

garder quelque chose pour la bonne bouche

to keep something up one's sleeve

Il garde toujours une histoire de son service militaire pour la bonne bouche.
He always keeps a story about his army days up his sleeve.

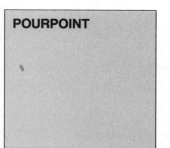

POURPOINT

à brûle-pourpoint

suddenly, without warning

Le Député s'est arrêté au beau milieu de son discours et, à brûle-pourpoint, il a dit qu'il allait abandonner la politique.
The Congressman stopped right in the middle of his speech and, without warning, he said he was going to leave politics.

Origin: **"A brûle-pourpoint" originally meant "at point blank range,"** i.e., so close that the bullet would burn ("brûler") the victim's doublet ("pourpoint").

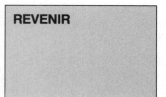

REVENIR

ne pas en revenir

to be unable to get over something (through surprise)

Je n'en reviens pas: trois livres pour le prix d'un! Quelle affaire!
I can't get over it: three books for the price of one! What a bargain!

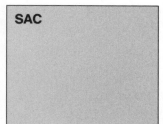

SAC

la main dans le sac

red-handed

On le soupçonnait depuis longtemps, et hier il a été pris la main dans le sac. Monsieur Brun l'a vu se servir dans la caisse.
They had suspected him for a long time and yesterday he was caught red-handed. Monsieur Brun saw him help himself from the cash register.

72. THOROUGHNESS, EFFICIENCY

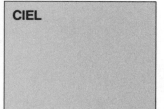

CIEL

remuer ciel et terre

to leave no stone unturned

Les gendarmes ont remué ciel et terre pour retrouver la petite Yvette disparue du domicile de ses parents depuis dimanche.
The police have left no stone unturned in their efforts to find little Yvette, who has been missing from her parents' home since Sunday.

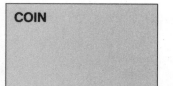

COIN

dans tous les coins et recoins

in every nook and cranny

J'ai cherché dans tous les coins et recoins. Impossible de retrouver ce billet de cinq cents francs.
I've looked in every nook and cranny. I just can't find that five hundred franc bill.

COUTURE

examiner quelque chose sous toutes les coutures

to examine something from every angle

Avant de prendre une décision, examinez la question sous toutes les coutures.
Before you make a decision, examine the question from every angle.

POT

découvrir le pot aux roses (coll.)

to get to the bottom of it

Quelqu'un maquille les comptes. L'inspecteur des impôts a dit au directeur qu'il a bien l'intention de découvrir le pot aux roses.
Someone has been tampering with the accounts. The tax inspector has told the manager he intends to get to the bottom of it.

73. TIME

CHIEN

entre chien et loup

in the twilight

Entre chien et loup, ce vieux château semble encore plus lugubre.
In the twilight this old castle looks even more somber and threatening.

Origin: **For the traveler it was once vital to be able to distinguish between a dog and a wolf on his journeys. This task became particularly difficult at dusk.**

FLEUR

dans la fleur de l'âge

in the prime of one's life

La maladie l'a emporté dans la fleur de l'âge. C'était un brillant médecin. Quelle perte!
The illness claimed him in the prime of his life. He was a brilliant doctor. What a loss!

JEUDI

la semaine des quatre jeudis

never in a month of Sundays

Pourquoi as-tu prêté tant d'argent à François? Tu le reverras la semaine des quatre jeudis.
Why did you lend François so much money? You'll never see it in a month of Sundays.

de nos jours

nowadays

De nos jours pratiquement tous les jeunes couples sont dans leurs meubles. Fort peu habitent des appartements meublés.
Nowadays, almost all young couples are in a house of their own. Very few live in furnished apartments.

sous peu

before long, shortly

Sois patiente. Je suis certain que la lettre arrivera sous peu.
Be patient. I'm sure the letter will arrive before long.

Il est onze heures sonnées.

It's past eleven.

Je regrette mais nous devons partir à présent. Il est onze heures sonnées et je dois ramener notre baby-sitter chez elle.
I'm afraid we'll have to leave now. It's past eleven and I have to take our babysitter home.

par les temps qui courent

the way things are at the moment

Mon fils voudrait bien être apprenti, mais par les temps qui courent c'est peu probable. A cause de la récession les entreprises prennent si peu d'apprentis.
My son would like an apprenticeship, but the way things are at the moment it's unlikely he'll get one. Because of the recession companies are taking on so few apprentices.

tous les trente-six du mois

once in a blue moon (coll.)

A en juger par son apparence, il doit se laver seulement tous les trente-six du mois.
Judging from his appearance, he must only wash once in a blue moon.

▬▬ 74. UNDERSTANDING, INTERPRETATION ▬▬

ÊTRE

J'y suis. (coll.)

I get you. (coll.) I follow you.

Ah oui, j'y suis à présent. C'est à mon père, pas à moi, que vous voulez parler. Ne quittez pas.
Ah, now I follow you. It's my father, not me, you want to speak to. Hang on a moment.

PARTI

en prendre son parti

to have to accept something

Tu dois en prendre ton parti: tu n'es pas du tout faite pour être infirmière. Tu ne peux pas supporter de voir du sang.
You've got to accept it: you're just not cut out to be a nurse. You can't stand the sight of blood.

PIED

prendre au pied de la lettre

to take literally

Ne prenez pas au pied de la lettre tout ce que le patron dit. Il fait plus de bruit que de mal.
Don't take everything the boss says literally. His bark is worse than his bite.

TENIR

savoir à quoi s'en tenir

to know where one stands

Elle change si souvent d'avis qu'on ne sait jamais à quoi s'en tenir.
She changes her mind so often that you never know where you stand with her.

▬▬ 75. UNHAPPINESS, SADNESS ▬▬

ÂME

C'est à vous fendre l'âme.

It breaks your heart.

C'est à vous fendre l'âme de voir la cruauté de certains parents envers leurs enfants.
It breaks your heart to see the cruelty of some parents towards their children.

CAFARD

avoir le cafard (coll.)

to be down (coll.), *to have the blues*

Il a le cafard. Sa petite amie l'a quitté.
He's down. His girlfriend has left him.

Origin: **"Un cafard" is a cockroach. The word acquired the meaning of an obsessive idea and was then eventually associated with depression, possibly because of the image a cockroach conjures up of being a black, repulsive creature.**

CŒUR

Cela me fait mal au cœur.

It grieves me.

Cela me fait mal au cœur de te voir gaspiller tout ton argent.
It grieves me to see you wasting all your money.

NOIR

broyer du noir

to be down in the dumps (coll.)

Depuis la mort de sa mère il broie du noir.
Since his mother's death he's been down in the dumps.

VIF

piquer au vif

to cut to the quick

Vous l'avez piqué au vif quand vous l'avez accusé d'avoir menti.
You cut him to the quick when you accused him of lying.

76. WEATHER

CANARD

Il fait un froid de canard. (coll.)

It's freezing cold.

Mettez des vêtements bien chauds si vous sortez. Il fait un froid de canard.
Put on warm clothes when you go out. It's freezing cold.

CHIEN

un temps de chien (coll.)

foul/filthy (coll.) *weather*

Nous ne pouvons pas aller piqueniquer aujourd'hui — il fait un temps de chien.
We can't go for a picnic today—it's foul weather.

Origin: **Expressions with "de chien" are used to convey disgust or contempt. The French seem to have had a low regard for dogs at one time.**

CORDE

Il pleut des cordes. (coll.)

It's raining cats and dogs. (coll.) *It's raining buckets.* (coll.)

On ne peut pas jardiner aujourd'hui — il pleut des cordes. *We can't do any gardening today — it's raining buckets.*

77. WILLINGNESS, READINESS, AGREEMENT

CŒUR

de bon cœur

willingly

Je t'aiderai de bon cœur à finir ce travail, mais seulement si tu y mets du tien. *I will willingly help you to finish the job, but only if you pull your weight.*

CŒUR

si le cœur vous en dit

if you like

Reprenez du potage, si le cœur vous en dit. *Do have more soup, if you like.*

DIRE

si cela te dit

if you like

Si cela vous dit, nous pourrions aller au théâtre samedi prochain, à moins que vous ne préfériez aller au cinéma. *If you like, we could go to the theater next Saturday, unless you'd prefer to go to the movies.*

FAIRE

si cela ne vous fait rien

if you don't mind

Si cela ne vous fait rien, nous aimerions repousser notre visite au mois prochain. *If you don't mind, we would like to postpone our visit until next month.*

OREILLE

se faire tirer l'oreille

to need a lot of persuading

Ça y est! Il a accepté, mais il s'est fait tirer l'oreille. *Success! He's accepted, but he needed a lot of persuading.*

78. WORRY, ANXIETY

CHARBON

être sur des charbons ardents

to be like a cat on a hot tin roof (coll.), *to be on pins and needles*

Encore deux heures avant la publication des résultats; tous les candidats sont sur des charbons ardents.
Another two hours before the results appear; all the students are on pins and needles.

COUP

être aux cent coups

to be at one's wits' end

Sa mère est aux cent coups; Pierre aurait dû être de retour il y a plus de deux heures.
His mother is at her wits' end; Pierre should have been back more than two hours ago.

FAIRE

s'en faire

to worry

Ne t'en fais pas. Je suis sûr que tu réussiras ton permis de conduire.
Don't worry. I'm sure you'll pass your driver's test.

NERF

avoir les nerfs à fleur de peau

to be on edge

La moindre des choses l'irrite depuis sa dépression. Elle a les nerfs à fleur de peau.
The slightest thing irritates her since she's been depressed. Her nerves are on edge.

PAS

faire les cent pas

to pace up and down

Les couloirs de la maternité étaient pleins d'hommes qui faisaient les cent pas.
The corridors in the maternity hospital were full of men pacing up and down.

SANG

se faire du mauvais sang

to be in a real state (coll.), *to be all worked up*

Nous sommes sans nouvelles depuis huit jours et nous nous faisons du mauvais sang. Qu'a-t-il pu lui arriver?
We've had no news for a week and we're in a real state. What could have happened to him?

French Index

The French idioms and proverbs included in the book are listed here in alphabetical order of key words.
(Abbreviations: coll. = colloquial; prov. = proverb.)

C

D

E

F

G

H

I

J

K

L

M

S

T

English Index

This index lists, in alphabetical order of key words, English idiomatic expressions that have a direct French idiomatic equivalent in this book. Also included in the list are common English idioms that have no direct French idiomatic equivalent. These are marked with an asterisk.

(Abbreviations: coll. = colloquial; o.s. = oneself; prov. = proverb; s.o. = someone; s.t. = something.)

C

D

E

M

N

O

P

T

U

VOLUME to speak *volumes* for s.o.*

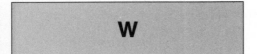

FOREIGN LANGUAGE BOOKS AND MATERIALS

Spanish
Vox Spanish and English Dictionaries
Cervantes-Walls Spanish and English Dictionary
Complete Handbook of Spanish Verbs
Guide to Spanish Suffixes
The Spanish Businessmate
Nice 'n Easy Spanish Grammar
Spanish Verbs and Essentials of Grammar
Spanish Verb Drills
Getting Started in Spanish
Guide to Spanish Idioms
Guide to Correspondence in Spanish
Diccionario Básico Norteamericano
Diccionario del Español Chicano
Basic Spanish Conversation
Let's Learn Spanish Picture Dictionary
Spanish Picture Dictionary
Welcome to Spain
Spanish for Beginners
Spanish à la Cartoon
El Alfabeto
Let's Sing and Learn in Spanish
Let's Learn Spanish Coloring Book
My World in Spanish Coloring Book
Easy Spanish Word Games and Puzzles
Easy Spanish Crossword Puzzles
Easy Spanish Vocabulary Puzzles
How to Pronounce Spanish Correctly

French
NTC's New College French and English Dictionary
NTC's Dictionary of *Faux Amis*
NTC's Dictionary of Canadian French
French Verbs and Essentials of Grammar
Getting Started in French
Guide to French Idioms
Guide to Correspondence in French
The French Businessmate
Nice 'n Easy French Grammar
French à la Cartoon
French for Beginners
Let's Learn French Picture Dictionary
French Picture Dictionary
Welcome to France
The French-Speaking World
L'Alphabet
Let's Learn French Coloring Book
My World in French Coloring Book
French Verb Drills
Easy French Crossword Puzzles
Easy French Vocabulary Games
Easy French Grammar Puzzles
Easy French Word Games
Easy French Culture Games
How to Pronounce French Correctly
L'Express: Ainsi va la France
Le Nouvel Observateur: Arts, idées, spectacles
Au courant: Expressions for Communicating in
   Everyday French

Audio and Video Language Programs
Just Listen 'n Learn: Spanish, French, Italian,
   German, and Greek
Just Listen 'n Learn PLUS: Spanish, French,
   and German
Conversational. . .in 7 Days: Spanish, French,
   German, Italian, Rusian, Greek, Portuguese
Practice & Improve Your. . .Spanish, French,
   and German
Practice & Improve Your. . .Spanish, French,
   and German PLUS
VideoPassport French and Spanish

German
Schöffler-Weis German and English Dictionary
Klett German and English Dictionary
Das Max und Moritz Buch
NTC's Dictionary of German False Cognates
Getting Started in German
German Verbs and Essentials of Grammar
Guide to German Correspondence
Guide to German Idioms
The German Businessmate
Nice 'n Easy German Grammar
German à la Cartoon
Let's Learn German Picture Dictionary
German Picture Dictionary
German for Beginners
German Verb Drills
Easy German Crossword Puzzles
Easy German Word Games and Puzzles
Let's Learn German Coloring Book
My World in German Coloring Book
How to Pronounce German Correctly

Italian
Zanichelli Italian and English Dictionaries
Basic Italian Conversation
Getting Started in Italian
Italian Verbs and Essentials of Grammar
Let's Learn Italian Picture Dictionary
My World in Italian Coloring Book
Let's Learn Italian Coloring Book
How to Pronounce Italian Correctly

Greek and Latin
NTC's New College Greek and English Dictionary
Essentials of Latin Grammar

Russian
Complete Handbook of Russian Verbs
Basic Structure Practice in Russian
Essentials of Russian Grammar
Business Russian
Roots of the Russian Language
Inspector General
Reading and Translating Contemporary Russian
How to Pronounce Russian

Hebrew
Everyday Hebrew

Japanese
Japanese in Plain English
Everyday Japanese
Japanese for Children
Japan Today!
Easy Hiragana
Easy Katakana
Easy Kana Workbook
How to Pronounce Japanese Correctly

Korean
Korean in Plain English

Chinese
Easy Chinese Phrasebook and Dictionary
Basic Chinese Vocabulary

Swedish
Swedish Verbs and Essentials of Grammar

"Just Enough" Phrase Books
Chinese, Dutch, French, German, Greek, Italian,
   Japanese, Portuguese, Russian, Scandinavian,
   Serbo-Croat, Spanish

PASSPORT BOOKS
a division of *NTC Publishing Group*
Lincolnwood, Illinois USA